From the book . . .

"By the time I was in second grade, I knew that people found me irritating. Their facial expressions told me as clearly as any verbal abuse. . . . I am not surprised that I began reaching out for help, although not in an open way. What does surprise me is the extreme manner in which I went about it: I began to steal."

"I was working on math problems and failing miserably. Instead of spacing the problems over the paper, I had bunched them all together in the top left corner, which only added to my confusion as I attempted to make some sense out of the mess of figures. Dad remembers me clenching my teeth and plunging ahead."

"Our courtship was anything but normal. As with everything else in me, there was little balance to my pursuit of my future wife. I courted her recklessly and impetuously."

"I am discovering that life is designed to be more than self and that we are created by God to be more than victims who wrestle with their own issues. We can be intimately involved in the lives of others. Parenthood is awesome in this regard. It . . . frees us from the narrow and crippling regard for th . . . me-generation meets its W . . .

UNC⬤MMON
Gifts

TRANSFORMING LEARNING
DISABILITIES INTO BLESSINGS

JAMES S. EVANS

Harold Shaw Publishers
Wheaton, Illinois

ISBN 0-87788-849-3

Edited by Joan Lloyd Guest

Cover design by David LaPlaca

Library of Congress Cataloging-in-Publication Data

Evans, James S. (James Stewart), 1959-
    Uncommon gifts : transforming learning disabilities into blessing / by
James Evans.
      p. cm.
    Rev. ed., with added chapters, of: An uncommon gift. 1983.
    ISBN 0-87788-849-3
    1. Evans, James S. (James Stewart), 1959-   . 2. Dyslexics—United States—
Biography. 3. Hyperkinesia—Patients—United States—Biography. 4. Christian
life—1960- I. Evans, James S. (James Stewart), 1959- Uncommon gift.
II. Title.
RC394.W6E9 1998
362.1'968553'0092   98-10408
[B]—dc21   CIP

05 04 03 02 01 00 99 98

10 9 8 7 6 5 4 3 2 1

Contents

Foreword

Being asked to write a foreword for your son's book is a challenge. We are hardly objective observers! We erupt with praise whenever we even think of Jamie, his wife, Kristy, and little Nate and Kelly who make up their family. So we begin by asking you to bear with us as you make allowances for our shameless parental pride.

The truth is, Jamie, the youngest of our four children, has blessed us and our family more than we could ever tell. We always are learning from him. Even as a little boy, he had a transparent, dazzling honesty about him; what he thought and felt was what you got. He was filled with love and exuberance for life and was a source of delight and joy to us as his parents.

At the same time, he was an incredibly active little guy, often making social situations tough. Early on, we thought his "busyness" simply was a family trait, but as time passed, "busy" became "hyper," and we sensed something was very different for Jamie.

Once he started school, we knew it was true. Reading was not only difficult for him; it was a nightmare! "Everyone else can read, why can't I? What's wrong with me?" he'd ask. His spelling lists were nonsense symbols.

"Jamie, you must watch the board more closely."

"But Mommy, that's what was on the board!"

Little did we know how true that was for him. Then came the suggestion from a discerning third-grade teacher that he have a "psychiatric evaluation." Our initial negative reaction gave way quickly to a kind of eagernesss and gratitude that perhaps at last some help was on the way. And it was.

The evaluation showed 1) hyperkinesis, 2) a difficulty with focus (Attention Deficit Disorder—ADD), and 3) moderate-to-severe dyslexia, a syndrome that few in our educational community understood. However, his doctor understood and helped Jamie to understand that he was not dumb but had a difficulty—a difference—in his brain's ability to perceive what his eyes saw. And Dr. Robert Carey, that wise doctor, helped us to understand as well. He confirmed that Jamie would need not only love and affirmation—this was a given—but he also would need boundaries and discipline. His progress would require after-school tutoring and three times as much energy and time on Jamie's part. And so his journey (and ours) began.

There were some tough years as Jamie learned to hunker down to discipline, tearfully sticking to what had to be done when nothing went right nor easily. Waves of self-deprecation, so familiar to the learning disabled, would rise from his turbulent sea of low self-esteem. But there were also incredibly sweet and encouraging successes. And we cheered them—each one—both great and small.

For one thing, we noticed a developing and quite astonishing capability in audial learning, as though what was lacking in one area was being compensated for in another. We also saw his eager, sweet nature working in his favor, sometimes masking his struggles, and at other times making them bearable. But most significant to us, we observed a spiritual sensitivity growing out of a relationship with his "friend-God" (Jamie's winsome way of referring to God). We felt this spiritual sensitivity was deepened by his personal encounter with pain. But that is Jamie's story to tell.

Let us simply say that whether you are the one with the learning difference, the parent of a special child, or the spouse of one who still struggles with the lingering remnants of a childhood disability, we wish we had some magic formula to offer all of you who read this book. If you yearn, as we did, to find answers, there is nothing we would like more than to be able to provide them. However, there is no "one-size-fits-all" approach to dealing with learning disabilities.

What we can tell you is that as we now look back over the years of struggle, our hearts fairly ache with gratitude. We marvel at the way God and Jamie together have made the promise of Romans 8:28, "All things work together for good," a reality.

But lest we make it sound as though rearing Jamie and three other highly energetic children was a snap for us, let us assure you, it was not. A privilege? Yes. Easy? No! Again and again during the "crunch years," we felt more was needed from us than we were able to give. And so, when at the end of our own resources, we learned to receive from God what we did not have. God, who loves all his children and is there in a special way for those who need him most, was our Pattern and our Provider for parenting. It was God's love that provided patience and constructive ideas. It was God's love that had "no limit to its endurance, no end to its trust, no fading of its hope" (1 Corinthians 13:7, Phillips).

Jamie's needs made us aware of our own need to trust God and not ourselves—and surely this is one of the most basic lessons God means for all of us to learn. Again, our son was teaching us. In concern for his destiny, we were finding our own.

And now, we commend our son's book to you. You will not find pat answers here, for there are none. But we do feel that whatever your circumstances, you will find in these pages insight, help, inspiration, and hope. It is our prayer that some of you will also find healing— and God—and that you will be able to say, with Jamie, that the learning challenges you would never have chosen have, in fact, become "uncommon gifts" in your life.

Colleen Townsend Evans
Louis Evans

A Postscript

As a dad and a still-learning adult, I should like to share some personal notes. I am so grateful to Jamie for what he is doing for so many of us hounded by dyslexia, attention deficit disorders, learning disabilities and differences, and the accompanying anger that goes along with these syndromes. "Us?" Yes, I am one too, although for decades I did not know it.

Two tracks are helping me: first, as a dad, I watched Jamie go through this struggle. In those early days it was his struggle and I was there with Colleen helping as God enabled us, but I did not see any application to myself. Now, in the second track as an adult, I am understanding much about myself through personal conversations with Jamie, but largely through his writings.

I remember the pain of sitting at my desk vainly trying to concentrate on my ninth-grade homework, despite the unbearable longings to be outside in physical activity or up in my room building model airplanes. Later, I recall the agony I felt during my doctoral studies as I would try vainly to control compulsive drives to design a camera tripod head or to make something with my hands. I remember the look of deep disappointment in Colleen's face when she would discover me lost in these distractions, rather than working on my unfinished dissertation.

I remember the anger and confusion in other people when I would fly off impulsively in some direction unexpected by my professional colleagues; my embarrassment of forgetting details in events which others assumed that I, as the pastor, should remember. And yet, in spite of those "glitches," I felt I had a lot to give in the churches I served, which proved to be the case.

For years I have struggled with eruptions of anger, exhibiting an irascibility when actions or time were frustrated, muttering self-deprecations. Where did this anger come from? Was it my family of origin? I could not find a basis for it there.

Now as I reread this book, insight is dawning. I am getting some perspective, primarily through Jamie's experience and his sharing. If only I had read this book decades earlier! I would have known who I was in my hyperactivity and impulsive distraction. I would have understood my anger at being a "dummy," a favorite expression for myself when I would goof up. I could have helped others to understand and cope with my behavior. I would have been quicker to drop my denial and defensiveness, to make the pocket lists for every hour of the day, and to control impulsive distractions. Yes, if only I had known what I know now, thanks to my son—my chest-bumping companion in "muscular Christianity" and my teacher/mentor.

This is why I wanted to write this postcript to the foreword, to encourage some of you—young or old—to read this book and see if it applies to your situation. Colleen and I have gained so much through Jamie's struggles, his perceptions, and his writings. We hope you will, as well.

Thank you, Jamie, for all you are, and for your uncommon gift.

LHE

Preface

Fourteen years have passed since the first edition of this book came out. In this edition I have revised and continued the story, now including my early adulthood and marriage.

This is more than a story about me. It is about millions of Americans, most of them males, who have learning disabilities. I am only one of them.

I have dyslexia, attention deficit, and hyperactivity. I read slowly, I stutter, I am a disaster in math. I was kept back a year in school, but I am not dumb. I am as restless and energetic as an Irish setter in a field, but I am not to be pitied. We who have learning disabilities don't need pity, but we do need. We need desperately.

During our early years we will not be good students. Our energy will drive many of you to consider us obnoxious and label us "behavior problems." But equip us at an early age to fight our battles, give us encouragement when others criticize, teach us to develop discipline, and harness our pain to help us reach a future goal, and we will not disappoint you.

Each individual with learning dyslexia is afflicted in various and unpredictable ways. Some have trouble seeing the words of a sentence in the correct order, others may not be able to orient what they think they see on a page with any coherent meaning, while still others may interchange letters such as *b* and *d* and spell phonetically. My particular brand of dyslexia is moderate in degree and visual in nature, although it also affects my motor coordination on occasion. I interchange letters, which considerably slows my reading and especially my comprehension rate. It also affects my mathematical ability; beyond long division I am lost.

Dyslexia in my case—and in many others'—is coupled with attention deficit with hyperactivity. I am continually in motion and alert to all stimuli around me. Thus, being easily distracted and already an uncontrollably active force within the classroom, I presented my teachers with a double challenge. Needing to listen more carefully to the spoken word, because I lacked perception in the area of reading, I was yet unable to sit still and concentrate for more than a few minutes at a time. I drove many well-intentioned instructors up the wall.

I was born with symmetry of the brain, often linked to dyslexia, which affects motor coordination and often causes stuttering. I exhibit both to a limited degree. To make a complicated description as simple as possible, symmetry of the brain occurs when the left lobe is not sufficiently dominant over the right. The left side of the brain controls articulation and motor coordination; it interjects the thoughts and concepts of the right side, forming speed and movement, among other things. In the ensuing battle for dominance, energy is expended, and when I come under mental or physical pressure, the high level of energy floods my nervous system.

Under such stress, my sentences get jumbled and the brain signals going to my left and right hands become confused. Suddenly I am clumsy in my movements and flustered in my communication attempts. Learning how to deal with these symptoms has been a major educational process in my life and in the lives of my family members, my teachers, several imaginative doctors, and some very special friends. By no means do I regret the experience. In many ways, my learning disabilities have made possible a rare, although often painful, blessing.

A blessing, yet a pain? In my vocabulary the terms are not mutually exclusive. I make no bones about my faith:

I'm a Christian and this book is written from a Christian's peculiar perspective on the world. I don't believe that pain has to be an enemy; it can be an enduring teacher. Learning disabilities do not have to be a handicap; they can become a force for discipline and sensitivity within the person afflicted. This perspective enables the person to survive, to grow, and even to surpass the other children and adults around him or her.

Those of us with learning disabilities must choose at an early age not to be defeated, or we will surely fail; we must choose to learn, or we will surely be left behind. That is our perspective; the choice is that simple. It is a black-and-white decision that only we can make. There will be no early rewards. We will have to learn to see life as many long-term goals, and be satisfied with bread today in the hope of enjoying a more abundant meal in the future.

I have written this book to help other people with disabilities to cope with the challenges they will have to face if they want to reach their full potential. I have also written it for anyone who faces a long-term hardship and wants to learn how self-discipline can help him or her get through the rough times.

Finally, I have written the book for those who know someone with a learning disability, especially if that person is a member of their family. Their sustained positive attitude is vital to that person's re-education process, and particularly to his or her self-esteem. It is my hope that this book will be a training tool for those who will have to spend the rest of their lives with us.

CHAPTER 1

Discovering I'm Different

La Jolla in Spanish means "the jewel" or "the pit"—take your pick. I was brought up there, and for me it was a little of both. I saw incredible beauty all around me, whether I was skin-diving under ten feet of water off the shore tidal pools or running through miles of sandstone canyons. I grew up a very loved child with affirming, supportive parents, and in that sense La Jolla was the jewel. But the pit was there, too. In La Jolla I learned what it meant to be lonely despite all the parental love I was given. It was there that I discovered I was different from my schoolmates, and I didn't like it. Something in me wasn't good, and it hurt.

I would become confused and talk in stutters, my mouth going so fast I couldn't control it. People were continually telling me to "settle down" or to "speak slowly." They would command, "Pay attention!" Couldn't they see I was going as slowly as I could and listening as hard as I could? Couldn't they see I didn't mean to get into trouble or break things, even though I always did? Try as I might, I never saw one of my spelling tests put up on the reward board. I never brought home a gold star to show my parents. I never could understand why my teacher would pick up my test paper, glance at it, and walk away with sadness in her face. She always smiled when she read what the girl next to me was writing. I began to think I was dumb and not a very good person.

I was born on June 1, 1959, in Los Angeles, but most of my early memories revolve around the beach town of La Jolla, just north of San Diego, where my family moved when I was four years old. Not long after my birth it had become apparent that I was, in some way, different. My hyperactivity was irrepressible (in my case, the dyslexia did not surface until later) and my enormous expenditure of energy presented my family with quite a challenge. For a long time they assumed I was exhibiting much of the same physical drive that was so visible in my father and even more so in my grandfather. Hyperkinesia, however, is not merely a lot of activity; it is perpetual motion, a seeking of stimulation through all the senses. It is a *need* and not simply a habit that can be turned off.

PEOPLE WERE CONTINUALLY TELLING ME TO "SETTLE DOWN" OR TO "SPEAK SLOWLY."

Even when I was lying in my crib, I had to exert energy. Why else were there bars on the crib if they were not meant to be rattled? The mobile dangling above my head moved; therefore, it had to be continually investigated. My energy was so intense that sleep was impossible until complete exhaustion overtook me. I have been told that I used to bounce my head against my pillow for hours until I was so thoroughly drained of energy that I would fall asleep. It was as if I had been designed to run like an engine with its throttle fully open, and only when I ran out of fuel could I come to a standstill.

Trying to help me fall asleep on a family trip was a real problem for everybody. Mom would take over the wheel and in her sternest voice declare a moratorium on wrestling, which always brought glee to my brothers' and sister's faces. My oldest brother, Dan, and my sister, Luanda, would get up front with Mom, and Tim, my next older brother, would sit beside Dad in the backseat. I would be placed in a portable crib in the rear of the old station wagon (before the days of seat-belt laws). Towels were propped along the crib edge to block out my view of the passing world because I was so easily distracted by moving stimuli. I kept trying to stand up to see what was going on, and Dad would gently but firmly put his big hand on my body to make me lie down. Then he would rock me back and forth, never allowing me to pop my head above the crib level to look out the windows. Sometimes it took hours of Dad's gentle pressure and rocking to settle me down to the point of sleep.

My mother, besides being an exceptional beauty, has the gift of patience. At home she would spend hours rocking me back and forth in a big old stuffed rocker, trying to calm me down. She has

NOT LONG AFTER MY BIRTH IT HAD BECOME APPARENT THAT I WAS, IN SOME WAY, DIFFERENT.

an impressive repertory of songs, and these, coupled with the rocking motion of the chair, were more successful than anything else in quieting me. But let there be one sound or the slightest unusual movement, and I'd be up and ready to go, which meant the entire procedure would have to begin all over again.

I wasn't mischievous, but I was inquisitive. If it moved, I had to investigate. Unfortunately, for most people that distinction was hard to make.

They fascinated me, those two gleaming silver poles upon which the giant above me supported himself. At the age of one year and a few months, all that mattered to me was investigating those poles that moved as my parents' massive friend moved. My parents called him "Paul." He had been crippled by polio, and sometimes after he visited us, my parents would marvel at the way Paul got around. My father would often comment about Paul's tremendous upper body strength and his fine voice that was such an asset to our church choir. At six feet two and a solid two hundred pounds, my father was not a small man, but Paul was even larger in the top part of his body. His chest and arms bulged against his suit, the thin material unable to hide the powerful muscles underneath it. Yet the man's legs seemed tiny, almost child sized, by comparison. Of course, none of that mattered to me; I was interested only in those silver poles.

I crawled toward them, making a beeline for the left crutch. It didn't yield to my first grasp and only gave way after much tugging. It was still attached to the giant's powerful arm above me. My curiosity still not satisfied, I grabbed again and succeeded in loosing the crutch from the floor—but not from the arm. The arm would not let go. More tugs brought more resistance, and my curiosity and excitement rose simultaneously. Suddenly I saw the soft rug underneath me disappearing. Someone was picking me up, lifting me to the giant's shoulder level. Paul was saying something to my parents and attempting to regain his balance at the same time. He blurted angry words to the effect of "controlling that boy!" The living room quickly disappeared from my view, and I found myself back in my familiar crib in the nursery. The bars around me and the mobile above my head couldn't hold my attention the way the silver poles had, but for the time being they would have to do.

My hyperactivity at that early age was a novelty to most people and was accepted by my parents as healthy. Only rarely did I anger someone with my activity, but when I did, I was not punished. My parents assumed that I would grow out of my energetic stage, just as my father had done. I think he, too, must have been hyperactive, but not to the degree I was.

There is a genetic connection between hyperactivity and learning disorders, although I don't know how evident they were in past generations of my family. My grandfather on my father's side was a frequent visitor to our house. He stood six feet four and had an authoritative voice but a gentle touch. I am told that during my crawling days I moved very fast on all fours, exploring every corner, touching every fixture within reach, causing my parents considerable fear when I tried to probe electrical sockets with a bobby pin. Restraining me was useless, so they watched me carefully.

On one of my expeditions I came upon a large pair of legs stretched across our living room floor. They belonged to my grandfather, who had just made himself comfortable while talking to my father. The legs were an irresistible attraction to my curious nature—and they were constantly moving! I attacked the right leg and hung on, bouncing from it to the left leg as I suddenly found myself rolling across the floor. I returned for a repeat performance and again and again assaulted the massive legs. My grandfather was trying to relax after a long day driving through rush-hour traffic, and serving as a jungle gym for his grandson was not what he had in mind. Drawing his abused legs back in frustration, he complained to my father, "What's the matter with this boy?"

LIKE ME, GRANDPA FOUND IT ALMOST IMPOSSIBLE TO SIT ABSOLUTELY STILL.

My father, who had been watching the David and Goliath contest quietly, said, "There's nothing wrong with him, Dad. He's just like you, that's all."

I've been told that after that encounter Grandpa and I developed a very special relationship, which lasted until his death shortly after my twenty-second birthday. Like me, Grandpa found it almost impossible to sit absolutely still. I used to find it consoling when I caught myself kicking my legs back and forth under my grandparents' dinner table and peeked under the table to find both my father's and my grandfather's legs moving back and forth in the same nervous pattern.

The first signs of dyslexia began to appear while we were living in Los Angeles, up in the dry hills of Bel Air. Many of our neighbors had built swimming pools in their backyards, but few had bothered to fence these in. At an early age we children were allowed to wander about the area with our playmates because my mother believed that too much time indoors was unhealthy for her energetic offspring. My older brothers and sister had taken to the outdoor life well, but before allowing them such freedom my parents had taught them to swim. There were many horror stories about young children drowning in a neighbor's pool, and my folks were determined not to allow their children to add to the tragic statistics. Dan, Tim, and Luanda were taught to swim almost before they could walk. They loved the water and showed no fear of my father's firm and careful instruction. It was expected that I would follow their example and brave the water for my swimming lessons. What was expected and what happened were not the same thing.

"Cokie [my mom's nickname], bring Jamie here. I'm ready for him now," the big man in blue trunks called, standing in the shallow end of our neighbor's pool. It was a brilliant spring day, and the usual morning smog had failed to materialize. Freeing myself from my mother's protective grasp, I teetered to the pool's edge, reaching for my father's outstretched hands. The dark hair on his muscular arms was turned temporarily blond by the sun; his big hands were callused from shoveling the foundation for our new patio. Jumping, I threw myself into his waiting arms and held fast to his neck. The wet stuff below me was scary and I wanted to keep as high up on his shoulder as I possibly could.

"Daddy, carry me on shoulder," I demanded, hoping for a ride. "No, Jamie, it's time for a swimming lesson. We're going to learn how to doggy paddle—won't that be fun?" he began. I didn't know what the "doggy paddle" was, and if it had anything to do with the wet stuff below me, I wanted nothing to do with it. I made my feelings known, grasping for the edge of the pool, but it was rapidly moving farther away. Turning me around, my father held me at arm's length, dangling my feet into the cool water. Squealing, I struggled to climb back on his shoulder. Our overweight dog was being helped into the deep end by my oldest brother, while my father was telling me to watch. Apparently I was supposed to learn from our dog, but as she slowly paddled around the pool simultaneously lapping up water, I cried out to my mother for rescue. It was too late. Dad was explaining the fundamentals of the dog paddle to me and wanted my attention.

"Jamie, make your hands go up and down, just like the doggy did with her paws. Do the same with your feet. Now try it, son," Dad instructed. Kicking, I tried my best, but was more intent on getting back to the edge than paddling farther from it. I screamed that I wanted out, but my cries went unheard. A new DC-8 streaked low over the house, making a thunderous racket and drowning out my squeals. My brothers, mouths wide open, were transfixed by the sight. Dan shouted that he could see the TWA insignia on the tail. The plane turned and headed for the Los Angeles airport, its bright metalwork gleaming as it rocketed out of sight. Again turning to my mother for rescue, I yelled that I wanted out, but she was trying to readjust my brother's shorts to their right position. (Tim was forever getting them twisted ninety degrees.)

"Now here we go, Jamie," Dad commanded. Water slowly came up to my chin as he lowered me into the pool. Struggling, I attempted to perform what I had been told to do, but found water flooding into my nose and mouth, making me sputter and cough. The next several attempts ended in similar failure. I began to cry. I could tell that my father was beginning to lose his patience by the sharp tone in his voice as I choked and screamed. I vaguely remembered a similar lesson only days before, ending in my refusal to go near the white rock-lined edge of the pool.

"Jamie, don't struggle. Just do as you're told. Now paddle just as our dog did and you'll be fine." Kicking with all my might, I tried to free myself from my father's grasp.

As far as I was concerned, the lesson was over. Every time I tried to paddle I got water in me.

I felt myself being carried to the edge and handed to my mother, her flowered one-piece bathing suit bright in the sun. "Louie, he may be a little slower than the others. Let's give him another week," she defended me.

Dad was exasperated. "Honey, it's important that he, especially, learn to swim. The way he toddles about, we're lucky to be able to keep him in the state. I don't want Jamie ending up a statistic. That's the kind of tragedy we can prevent."

My father is a preacher and a teacher by profession, and he is gifted in both those areas. Even in his personal approach to his children, he creates an aura of warm authority. But somehow when he told me to swim, I could not obey him. Somewhere in our communication there was a missed connection, and I could not bring my arms and legs under my control. We tried many more times, Dad and I, always ending in failure, and after all these years my father still looks back upon that experience with pain, blaming himself for losing patience. He wasn't at fault; neither was I. I was simply unable to co-ordinate my body movements and therefore sank like a rock. As a result, I developed a fear of the water. It wasn't until some years later that I finally learned to swim at the YMCA.

My memories are clearer after we moved to La Jolla. I don't like many of the feelings I can recall. I was lonely and confused. For some reason, other children my age were reluctant to spend time with me. I know now that they were unnerved by my hyperactivity. I began to cre-ate an intricate fantasy world that included not only playmates but clubs of which I was the leader. If I couldn't be a success in the outer world, I was certainly going to be one in my own inner realm. It's not that fantasizing is unusual for children, but I spent far more than the usual amount of time in that unreal world. I felt affirmed by the people in it, while the real world offered precious little affirmation aside from my parents' enduring support. It was my only way of escaping from the question that kept going through my mind: *Why am I different?*

Eventually my dream world began to change. I wanted so much to be liked by the other children in our neighborhood; I wanted my brothers to play with me; I craved any attention paid to me by others; and when I couldn't reach these goals, I began to get very angry. My inner world was no longer a peaceful place to be.

FOR SOME REASON, OTHER CHILDREN MY AGE WERE RELUCTANT TO SPEND TIME WITH ME.

I learned very early that to show anger in destructive ways only got me into trouble. Breaking my brothers' models and talking back to my parents were not tolerated for a moment in our household. But in my fantasy world, anger could have full vent. I could become the captain of a mighty warship and destroy the Nazi raiders (who just happened to resemble the kids from around the block who had shunned my company). At the same time, I began to build models, which enhanced my daydreaming. Now I could actually build a mighty warship as well as be its captain!

Internalizing my anger was a harmful habit; it increased my inner tension and made communication even more difficult. Yet there was no denying the emotions I was feeling. Anyone with a learning disability, whether diagnosed or not, will feel anger and must find a way to vent it. I repressed it by fantasizing, but to repress it further would have done great damage. I was dealing in the best way I could with forces I did not understand and could not control. At least my dream world allowed me to release some of my confusion and frustration. I've often thought that it would be a good idea for parents to explore this part of a child's life by trying to talk to him or her about it. If parents can enter the child's dream world and find out who inhabits it, they will gain a much better understanding of the child's reactions to some of the hurts in life. This dream world is actually a direct line into the most sensitive area of the child's personality, and that is a worthwhile area to explore. Of course, I didn't know that then. It took me years to find it out.

One of the factors that added to my confusion as a child was my ungainliness. I was unusually big for my age, and my lack of motor coordination made me stumble around like a young colt with more energy than agility. This poor coordination is caused by too much symmetry in the makeup of the brain. For instance, under pressure to perform athletically, my nervous system would be flooded with energy, and my brain signals would get confused. Sometimes I found it difficult to quickly distinguish my right leg from my left, which in turn made it difficult for me to coordinate my movements.

In elementary school my clumsiness became a problem. I remember the Torrey Pines Elementary School, situated above the main part of town on an undeveloped section of Scenic Drive. The sage and canyons were disturbed then only by our solitary neighborhood. There was plenty of running space for an energetic loner like me to explore. When the businessmen of La Jolla began investing money into the area to develop sizable tracts of land, this pro-

vided even more adventure for me. I spent days roaming
about and playing on the massive earth-moving machin-
ery. The utility trenches provided ready-made forts for
creating intricate fantasies. While these building sites
were fraught with potential dangers, I found them havens
of interest and activity.

At exercise time we were encouraged to join the upper
classes in our activities. The classes were divided into
two large teams, which were split into smaller sections.
One of our games was dubbed "kill ball," and we couldn't
get enough of it. Two or three balls were used at one
time in a sort of multilayered dodge ball. It was a complicated game in theory, with a simple objective: hit the
other team and don't be hit by them. Team A would
sandwich Team B and in turn Team B would sandwich
Team A. What made the game most exciting was that a
ball could come from either direction, and the blind-side
hits could knock an unprepared player right off his feet.
Innumerable pairs of glasses and retainers were lost to
this game, and eventually it was banned; but when I was
in school it was the hottest game going.

I look back on the game with mixed emotions. As a
player, I usually occupied the shooter's position. I rarely
qualified for the more prestigious shooter-runner spots;
they were reserved for those with agile bodies and quick
reflexes, and I had neither at the time. When I got the
ball, I had little chance of hitting my opponents, but I
certainly had strength. Once I recall releasing the ball
and totally missing my anticipated target. Failed again.
Suddenly someone was pounding me on the back for my
excellent shot. My shot had scored a blind-side hit upon
the center of another guy's back. In throwing the ball so
hard across the court, I was bound to hit some unfortunate player, even if it wasn't the one I had aimed at.

Athletics is not governed by chance. If I was to compete successfully with my ten-year-old peers, I had to be consistently skillful, and I wasn't. I was forced to recognize my limitations in Little League baseball the following year. For two years I had been coached by my father in the B leagues and did fairly well under his patient discipline. But as I advanced into the A leagues with the rest of the third-graders, I found myself hopelessly outclassed. I could no longer ignore my awkwardness in comparison to my teammates, who were beginning to achieve a fairly strong command of the game. I gave up baseball that year, preferring to spend my afternoons on my own in the canyons or making models in my room.

The classroom presented a whole set of separate problems. On the athletic field I could at least vent most of my physical energy as I learned. In the classroom, I found it nearly impossible to concentrate, since I had to sit still and listen. For a hyperactive child, sitting still is a major undertaking in itself. Tack onto that the extra concentration needed for me to understand a task, and you can imagine the frustration both my teacher and I felt. Not realizing that I had a learning disorder, teachers tended to view me as a discipline problem. When one is treated as a discipline problem, one becomes a discipline problem, and I lived up to their expectations with all that was in me.

There were many horror stories told about me among the Sunday school teachers at church. I was the pastor's son, and one of the biggest headaches in the class! It wasn't that I was a bad kid. I didn't beat up on others or abuse the teacher, but keeping me still or quiet was next to impossible. My ever-positive mother called it "being busy," but my Sunday school teachers had another word for it: obnoxiousness. I can remember the day I was dragged and then carried from my second-grade church school class down to the office. Apparently I had finally

driven my teacher to distraction. He and I can laugh
about it now. When I saw him last, we did, but at the
time it happened, it was anything but funny. He never
taught again.

The message was coming across loud and clear: I was
different, and the difference was becoming less and less
tolerated. Looking back, I can thank my parents for continuing to affirm me. In their eyes I was not a discipline
problem, but a very special, busy son, and they kept re-
minding me of that. Youngsters who are dyslexic or hyperactive don't get a great deal of praise from the outside
world, so it is vitally important that they get it at home.
I did. And I gobbled up every bit of it.

CHAPTER 2

Asking for Help

In one way or another we all ask for what we do not have and feel we cannot live without. My sister recently gave birth to a baby girl who without fail lets the world know when she is hungry for food or attention. Unfortunately, as we mature, this type of spontaneous communication is discouraged by society. An adult does not wail until his intimacy needs are fulfilled; he has learned to communicate his needs more subtly through the "proper channels," which often results in repression. Anger is buried under politeness; hunger for affirming affection is well concealed beneath a fear of people; and thirst for a relationship with God is regularly denied by fear of fanaticism.

By the time I was in second grade, I knew that people found me irritating. Their facial expressions told me as clearly as any verbal abuse—and to this day I am keenly aware of the slightest sign of boredom or impatience when I am with someone. I am not surprised that I began reaching out for help, although not in an open way. What does surprise me is the extreme manner in which I went about it: I began to steal.

Imagine yourself walking through a forest filled with friends and enemies. The friends are armed with feathers, and as you travel along the forest path, they throw them toward you in the form of affirming praise. These feathers are then picked up by your mind and put into a pillow or cushion wrapped around your body—let's call it "the cushion of self-worth." As the miles pass, more and more feathers accumulate from family, friends, and individual achievements, creating a protective barrier about you.

Also along the forest path are your enemies. They may be actual enemies in the flesh, or embarrassing actions, or errors you have committed. Each one is armed with a single arrow. As you walk by them, they fire their arrows toward your cushion, and they never miss. Thankfully, your cushion of self-esteem can easily withstand the attack. Because the arrows expend much of their energy on the way, most never actually penetrate your protective cushion. But each arrow must be extracted, and in the process a few of the protective feathers fall out, thus deflating your cushion.

The aim of this forest stroll is to acquire more feathers than arrows, and as long as you can pick up enough feathers there is no real cause for alarm. But let the number of feathers fall to the level where your cushion can no longer protect you from incoming arrows, and your emotions send you a message that all is not well—more affirmation is desperately needed to reinforce your cushion. These warning signals in a mature adult who has not been adversely affected by society's strictures against "wearing one's heart on one's sleeve" will translate into a need for close contact with friends who affirm and thus "add feathers to your cushion." Unfortunately, many adults feel that such a reaching out is not acceptable. This restraint is especially true of Americans, bred as we are in the pioneer spirit of rugged individualism. Many of us must therefore find other means to fill our damaged cushions, and often these means are unhealthy: heavy drinking, drugs, abusive behavior, and extramarital sex, to name but a few. They are substitutes for real affirmation, and in most cases they only dull the pain of the arrows for a moment, without adding any real substance to the cushion of self-worth.

A child's emotions behave in a similar manner. They send the necessary danger signals to the brain, but the child does not yet have the relational ability to reach out for the healthy affirmation needed even if it is available. So the child resorts to other methods to ask for help.

> BECAUSE I WAS SLOW IN THE CLASSROOM AND AWKWARD, A LOT OF NEGATIVE REACTIONS FROM PEERS DUG INTO MY SENSITIVE FLESH.

Because I was slow in the classroom and very awkward socially, a lot of negative reactions from peers and siblings penetrated my cushion and dug into my sensitive flesh. There they festered, causing a slowly growing image of myself as a "bad" person. I wanted my friends and my teachers to be glad I was there—and they didn't seem to be.

I could see them lined up on my father's clothes rack in the corner of my parents' bedroom. They glistened on the wood frame: six quarters, assorted dimes, and nickels. It was my father's orderly habit to place his spare coins on his clothes rack whenever he changed from his office

clothes into the jeans and T-shirts he wore around the
house as he and my older brothers worked on the addition to our overcrowded quarters. The smell of sawdust
and cement mingled with the orange blossoms and ever-
present ocean mist that characterized La Jolla. It was early
afternoon and my mother had left the bedroom door ajar.

As I peeked in, I could see no signs of movement and
judged the coast to be clear. My brothers were off on
their daily surfing excursions to the nearby Shores beach
or to the more distant Blacks beach, whose surfing area
was known for its cliffs and sizable waves. My sister,
Andie, was still in school. Dad must have been at church.
There was only Mom to worry about, and she was wrist
deep in preparing a turkey for our dinner. The only wit-
ness to my act would be the seventh member of our family, our dog, Nikki, named after the brave Alaskan husky
but far more benign. As I entered the bedroom, Nikki
lazily eyed me from her spot in the afternoon sun, in
front of the sliding glass door leading to the garden area
Dad had recently constructed. I moved toward the
wooden rack, and Nikki rested her head on the carpet,
continuing her siesta.

My eight-year-old's logic told me that to take the
whole pile of coins would attract attention, and Dad's
wrath was to be avoided at all costs. I decided to take
ninety cents, about half the total amount. That would
more than pay for the model I had my heart set on down
at the local 7-Eleven store. I grabbed the coins and quietly left the room, being careful to leave the door as I
had found it. As I walked down the hall toward my bedroom, a sense of guilt came over me. It increased as I
approached the kitchen, where my mother was cooking.
But in moments I was out the door leading from my room
to the side street. I remember the guilt fading as I brought
the model back and began to put it together. Soon I was
absorbed in the play world I had created, strafing enemy

airfields with my newly finished toy plane and mentally building hangars and mock runways for it.

It didn't take long for me to learn that my father was more aware of his change than was my mother. Shifting strategy, I left the coins where they were and took an occasional dollar bill from my mother's purse. I would generally follow the same routine: wait for Dad to be away at church while Mom was in the kitchen or out doing the wash, and then go quickly into their room and take what I thought I could without being noticeably greedy. I was becoming convinced that stealing did indeed pay.

My opportunities seemed limitless in store-filled La Jolla. Susan's Toy Store was a model maker's dream, with its major line of ships, tanks, and airplanes to choose from, and plenty of narrow shelves and aisles to hide a nine-year-old's pilfering. I could never bring myself to shoplift outright, but I was willing to open a large model's box and place a number of smaller items inside it so that I paid only for the large item and walked out with the rest.

Even the church wasn't safe from my thieving.

The deacons would trustingly place a bowl in the narthex for donations to help pay for the literature displayed there. Leaving my Sunday school class early, I would head toward the main sanctuary, where my father was preparing to deliver his sermon. Peering from behind the flowering shrub beside the main entrance to the nave, I would wait for the last of the ushers to leave the narthex and enter the sanctuary, closing the huge wooden doors behind them. It was almost time. A snail traveled slowly across the leaf of a plant in front of my foot. Raising my foot to crush him, I paused momentarily. He was leaving a moist trail behind him as he traversed the broad-leaved bush, as if he were signing his name to it. On his shell I could see tiny swirls of brown and tan spiraling out. A janitor crossed the lawn in front of me carrying the bags of cubed bread for Communion. (I loved to make little wads out of the cubes during our monthly Communion service; it made excellent spitballs that would stick fast to any target.)

The boom of my father's voice came from within the church as he started his sermon. It was time to make my move. I ran in a crouched position to the stairs that led to the narthex and peered into the chamber. The door was just now closing. All the ushers were gone. Carefully I climbed the stairs and tiptoed to the table at the far wall where the literature was displayed. On it was a bowl filled with quarters and dimes. They beckoned enticingly. As I was reaching for them, I was stopped by the squeak of one of the big oak doors opening—an usher was returning to get the offering plates stored in the adjacent closet. I quickly picked up a tract, pretending to read.

Returning with the plates, the usher smiled and called out softly: "What ya doing there, Jamie? Catching up on your Bible study?" Not waiting for my reply, he crossed to the rear of the nave, silently closing the doors behind him. *Who would suspect a pastor's son?* I thought. By the tone of my father's voice reverberating through the wall, I knew he was making his final point, so I had to work quickly. I scooped up a third of the change, about two dollars, and stuffed it into my pocket. Then I bounded down the stairs and was off, feeling very clever.

Incidents like this were not sporadic or isolated. I began to steal when I was eight, and it had become a habit by the time I was nine. This coincided with the increasing confusion my undiagnosed disability was causing. I am not excusing it with this explanation. I knew I was doing wrong. Nor can I claim ignorance as a shield; early on, my parents had taught me that honesty was a vital quality in a person. I didn't need more toys; I had more than enough, having inherited many from my brothers, and my weekly allowance enabled me to buy a model or two on a regular basis. However, later on it took a wonderful counselor only a few sessions to make sense of the question that had troubled me for years: Why did I steal so much at that time?

The counselor said I was crying out for help in the most available manner I could. My stealing, had I been caught, would have been a clear violation of everything I had been taught. It was more than a symptom of my low self-image; it was a signal flare illuminating the negative forces gnawing beneath my surface. I was saying to the outside world: "Look, stop and look, I'm acting bad, very bad, because I'm starting to believe I am bad, and a little boy isn't supposed to think that. Look at me! Can't you see your money missing? Can't you see the missing models and empty coin bowls? This is an alarm! The cushion is too thin to keep the arrows out any longer . . . Somebody, please look and help! It hurts in here, and it's not supposed to."

> I BEGAN TO STEAL WHEN I WAS EIGHT, AND IT HAD BECOME A HABIT BY THE TIME I WAS NINE.

CHAPTER 3

"You've Got a Problem"

Often the future of a young person with learning disabilities is decided for him or her at an early age. This child knows he has a problem, but he doesn't understand what it is. All too often, others don't, either; yet it is upon these others that the child's future development rests. An early diagnosis of the problem is the crucial first step: a psychologist must be consulted, and a plan for the child's retraining must be scrupulously followed by both the child and the parents. Unfortunately, that first step often isn't taken until too late in the child's life—or not at all.

I blame no one for failure to confront a child's disability. Parents assume a child's teacher is better equipped to distinguish between unruly behavior and something more serious. But in today's classrooms, overcrowding and discipline problems can so sap a teacher's energy that he or she has nothing left to expend on the extra demands of the "problem" student. If the parents don't recognize the need for diagnostic testing, then in many cases there will be none.

On the parents' side, there is the matter of pride: "Our child doesn't need to see a shrink—her problems aren't that bad!" This reluctance to confront the issue has doomed many a bright student who might otherwise have a chance to excel in life.

Compare, for example, the true accounts of two dyslexics, mine and that of a boy we'll call Stephen.

Stephen was from the well-to-do neighborhood in Cleveland, Ohio. His home was not modest and dominated the center of a spacious lawn and circular drive. He was the youngest son of an industrialist; his brothers before him had been keen successes in school, had gone on to Ivy League colleges, and had graduated well above the average of their classes. There seemed no reason why Stephen should not have followed in their footsteps, but from the beginning of his schooling he had proved to be different.

I BLAME NO ONE FOR FAILURE TO CONFRONT A CHILD'S DISABILITY.

His principal reported to his parents that, although Stephen was a likable child, he was doing poorly in his studies and was difficult to control. Stephen was not destructive or abusive; rather, he was "busy" and was often described as "not paying attention." His parents, remembering their other sons' successes, concluded that Stephen was simply a slow starter who with time and discipline would adjust to the rigors of academics. But Stephen didn't adjust. As his school failures increased and the difference between him and his classmates became more apparent, his behavior became a problem.

This was a critical period for Stephen. It was then that his parents might have noticed that his failures in school, coupled with increasing discipline problems, were his cries for help. But consider his parents' position: to have Stephen tested for an "abnormality" or "disability" would have required them to admit that there might be something wrong with their son—perhaps even a genetic defect inherited from one of them. This is difficult for many parents to accept, especially when their other children have been successful in school and proved to be very bright. Could we have given birth to a disabled child? they ask themselves. In any community this is a tough pill to swallow, but even more so in an upper-middle-class area where such disabilities aren't openly discussed and where children generally do well in school. In any event, Stephen was not tested. It was assumed that he would grow out of his difficulties and that with the proper discipline from his teachers he would succeed in school as his brothers had before him.

Stephen was passed from grade to grade, routinely doing poor work and becoming more of a nuisance for his instructors. He was fast turning into the bad sheep of his family. More than once his parents found drugs hidden in his room, and his companions were not the sort of boys who were interested in academic excellence. Yet for some reason his parents still did not get him help. Could it be that they were ashamed to admit they had a "problem child" who needed professional help? As a dyslexic, I find such reluctance hard to understand, yet it is apparently widespread. Stephen's school continued to pass him along until it was discovered during the spring of his senior year that he was reading at a second-grade level. One teacher finally had the foresight and courage to fail Stephen for his own good, forcing him to receive the summer-school training that might help him. But because of his undiagnosed dyslexia and lack of good study habits, Stephen never went beyond a high school education. He works near his home in an automobile assembly plant. He tightens bolts on the blocks as the engines pass by him, and one of these days he will be replaced by a robot. He continues to live at home and is accumulating a police record for a number of drug-related incidents. His family continues to believe that someday "he'll grow out of it."

Stephen's story is tragic. While I cannot blame all his problems on his disability or on his parents' unwillingness to have him tested, I feel certain that his life would have been radically different had he been given professional care and pushed to compensate for his handicap. Recently, under pressure from local authorities who can no longer look upon his misdemeanors as the pranks of a rambunctious boy, Stephen has been seeing a therapist. From a number of psychological tests it has been determined that he is a moderate-to-severe dyslexic. I can't help wondering what might have happened if those tests had been done years ago, before a young boy's life was shaped by the confusion and anger he experienced.

THANKS TO THE CONCERN— AND THE COURAGE—OF MY PARENTS, MY STORY TAKES A DIFFERENT TURN.

I have a lot in common with Stephen. I can identify with the frustration he must have felt in his early classroom and social experiences. I know his anger. I know the pain he felt looking at a sentence one word at a time and having none of it make sense to him, while others in his class read with ease. I know the shame of not being able to carry out instructions. And I know how the words "dumb" and "bad" can cut your insides to pieces when you start believing they might be true. But that is the extent of the similarities between Stephen and me. Thanks to the concern—and the courage—of my parents, my story takes a different turn. With their help and continued support, and with the help of some very special teachers and professionals, I was able to turn a handicap into a most uncommon blessing.

I climbed into the front seat of our wagon and waited for my mother to join me. She had received a phone call a moment earlier and said she'd be there as soon as she finished talking. "Sure, she'll be right here—last time she said that, it took fifteen minutes," I groaned to myself, settling into the bench seat for a long wait. There was one hope: my mother had promised to pick up my time-conscious father on our way to the pharmacy. Mom wouldn't want to be late picking up Dad, I thought, so she'd cut her conversation short. I was looking forward to browsing around the model-stocked shelves of the pharmacy in the Nautilus Building.

Picking a piece of the dashboard off its torn frame, I wondered who this Dr. Carrie was that Mom had been telling me about. Mom had said he was a pediatrician who had gone back to school to get his Ph.D. in psychiatry. He worked with children who had learning disabilities, and he was going to give me some tests. I was pretty sure that a pediatrician was a long way of saying "kids' doctor," but I had no idea what a psychiatrist was. In any event, I hoped he didn't use needles. My arm was still sore from the booster our family doctor had given me a week ago. I hated shots.

Two F-4 Phantoms screamed over our house, their tight formation and bomb racks marking them as Marine planes from the nearby Miramar air base. My dad had taught me how to identify them by their unique wings and tails. He said they were practicing for Vietnam— which was somewhere in Asia where my eldest brother, Dan, did not want to go.

Mom came running out of the house and quickly started the car, and we were on our way through the morning traffic of downtown La Jolla. It was a particularly sunny morning; the beachside streets were filled with wet-suited surfers coming from their early adventure with the waves and heading toward school. Slowing, Mom waved to a group of long-haired teenagers, their surfboards slung under their arms, friends of my brother Tim.

Picking Dad up at the church, we drove to the massive blue-and-white Nautilus office building. Much to my disappointment, we parked well away from the drugstore and close to the offices located on the other side of the building, next to a grove of eucalyptus trees.

Dr. Carrie was a gray-haired man sitting in front of a huge line of picture windows. His office smelled of old leatherbound books and paper, not like the doctor's office I had dreaded, but like my grandfather's study.

"Jamie, why don't you come with me into the playroom, where we'll talk and draw," Dr. Carrie said. "Your parents can stay here while we're doing that." As we walked through the soundproof door into the brightly colored, toy-strewn room, I looked back at my parents. Their faces were serious and they were holding hands.

Soon I was engrossed in play. "Now, Jamie, draw what you see me draw," the doctor instructed. He sketched a picture of a telephone-pole-like figure, which I drew as quickly as possible. Then he brought out cards with short words on them that I was to copy. While we drew, he asked me questions: "Do you like school, Jamie? Do you have fun with kids in your class?"

"No, I don't like my school. I do really bad at it, and there aren't many kids I play with. I'm better at playing with my models at home after school."

"Who do you play with when you're playing with your models?" he asked, this time showing me a word I couldn't make out but was told to copy anyway.

"I don't play with anyone usually. I go down to the beach and play there, or sometimes I play with Richard, across the street."

We were now drawing lines and boxes, all shapes and

sizes. I was beginning to enjoy the testing. Dr. Carrie was easy to talk to, and there were always games to play between the drawing and words. I was told to return the following Tuesday, at which time Dr. Carrie promised to teach me how to play chess.

The tests went on for about three weeks. I found chess a fun game, and while we played, the questions went on—about my brothers and sister, my home, my school, my teachers. Usually my mother drove me to my appointment and waited for me in the car, but on one rainy day I returned to the book-lined office after some time in the playroom and found both my parents waiting there. Dr. Carrie said he had some important test results he wanted to share with all of us. I tried hard to remember what tests he meant; all I remembered doing was playing chess and talking about school. Maybe he meant the lines he asked me to draw. Settling into a seat between my parents, I waited for the doctor to begin. He was selecting some papers from a stack in the corner of his desk. I tapped my feet on the chair leg opposite me, trying to push it across the floor. A look from my father told me that wasn't the sort of thing to do in an office, but I found it hard to sit still.

I HAD TO LEARN NEW WAYS TO TAKE IN INFORMATION AND ASSEMBLE IT IN MY BRAIN.

Seating himself, the doctor shuffled his papers. "Mr. and Mrs. Evans, and Jamie, I have the results here," he said. "As I thought, Jamie, you are a moderate dyslexic with hyperkinesia. In our tests you had difficulty copying the figures I had drawn."

Pulling his first sketch from the stack, he compared mine to it. I was surprised to see that they didn't look a bit alike.

"As you can see, Jamie has a perceptual difficulty. His hyperactivity adds to this disability by decreasing his attention span in the classroom. You tend to reverse letters and numbers, Jamie—that's just one part of what's called dyslexia. Your 'busyness' is part of hyperkinesia, or hyperactivity. That's why it's hard for you to be still. Most children, when properly diagnosed and treated, grow out of this learning disability by late adolescence. But it will take much work and discipline on your part, Jamie."

"Now, Jamie," he said, "I don't want you to think of yourself as stupid because of this. You're not. I taught you to play chess to gauge your IQ by means other than the written or visual tests. As far as I can tell, you're very bright. It's hard for you, though, to translate the information you take in perceptually to concepts you can retain."

So that's why I'm different, I thought.

I had to be re-educated, Dr. Carrie said. I had to learn new ways to take in information and assemble it in my brain. It was going to require tremendous energy from me, all of it directed toward a single goal: overcoming my disability. I had the intellectual means to do it; now I needed the will. I also needed all the help I could get.

I was told that discipline would become my watchword. I would have to learn by means of a great deal of repetition, and I would need tutors to help me strengthen my weaker areas. I would have to work much harder than the average student. Afternoon play would take second place to my studies, and homework was to be done without argument or procrastination. I wasn't told until later that it would take me five hours to do the amount of homework an average student could do in two.

So much for my dyslexic problems. There was still the matter of hyperactivity to address. True, the added discipline imposed by teachers specially trained to handle dyslexics would do much to control my irrepressible busyness, but that was a temporary remedy. I needed a more effective, long-range way to control the flood of energy that blocked my attention span.

Dr. Carrie told us about Ritalin, a drug that could slow me down by speeding up the portion of my brain that was designed to control my energy. How peculiar it was to consider taking a stimulant to slow me down, yet Ritalin had been successful in others, and it was worth a try in my case. My parents and I consented to use the drug on a trial basis.

I must add here that we were warned of possible side effects: I might lose my appetite, become a bit moody, and slow down to a greater degree than normal. My parents were concerned about the risks and discussed them with me, but in the end it was my decision. I took the Ritalin.

You may think it odd that my parents allowed me to make the decision. Wasn't that too much responsibility for a third-grader to handle?

No. If my dyslexia was going to be beaten, my only weapons would be hard work, discipline, and professional help; and the bulk of the fight would be mine. The choice was clear: either I fought or I failed. I might have had a child's disorder, but a child's response was not going to overcome it. I had to grow up in a very short amount of time. Recognizing that urgency, my parents began giving me large amounts of responsibility to prepare me for a more demanding way of life. The decision about Ritalin was only the beginning.

My parents also were painfully honest in their affirmation. I remember some of the talks we had shortly after the diagnosis.

"Dr. Carrie has discovered a problem in you, Jamie. It's called dyslexia," my father would explain. "That's why you've been having trouble with your friends and in school. Do you know what perception means? It means 'seeing' and you have difficulty 'seeing' letters properly in your mind. No, your eyes are fine; you won't need glasses. This kind of seeing is in your brain. Jamie, it will give you problems in school for quite some time, but you must remember one thing: *you are not dumb.* In fact, Dr. Carrie tells us that you are a very bright boy. But even bright boys have problems sometimes in school."

"Remember, Jamie," my father would add, "you're a smart boy, and with daily work you're going to beat this. You're going to change the way you see letters and words and numbers. Remember how often you've beaten me when we play chess? You know you're smart in chess, and with a lot of hard work you're going to be just as smart in school."

Gradually my confusion was clearing up, and I could see the enemy. There were years of struggle ahead of me, but that prospect was a relief compared to the dark doubts I had had for so long. I could do something about my situation, and I wouldn't be doing it alone. My parents would work with me; so would Dr. Carrie. And there would be others—even God.

During the years of my confusion, a lot of anger had been building up in me against God. I blamed him for my failure to measure up to my peers.

I remember once, when I was about eight years old, walking into a sunlit living room in a nearby house. I had been sent in by my mother to tell my sister we were ready to drive her home. I didn't know my sister was attending a prayer meeting for young people who had recently become Christians, but as I entered the room I heard them praying out loud. They seemed very intense and didn't notice me. Being a minister's son, I was ac- customed to prayer groups, yet I distinctly remember that I suddenly became frightened and angry that afternoon. I felt different from these kids. I could not love God, and I could not believe he loved me.

I did not change my mind about God immediately after Dr. Carrie's diagnosis. In fact, I was becoming very uncomfortable as more and more of the young people I knew in church and in our neighborhood began committing themselves to Christ. I felt a strange anxiety and dread at the thought that I was expected to follow suit. How could I? I was a stranger to the God who loved normal people.

> **I FELT DIFFERENT FROM THESE KIDS. I COULD NOT LOVE GOD, AND I COULD NOT BELIEVE HE LOVED ME.**

Every summer our family spent a few weeks at Camp Onogo in the mountains just above Lake Arrowhead, where our church conducted its annual family retreat. It was almost time for us to go, and I was wishing I could be left behind. I would have preferred anything to an encounter with God. I was afraid of what might happen.

I could barely make out the dusty, needle-strewn trail in front of me. Tears burned my eyes and dulled my vision. The dusk was settling over the forest, and off in the distance the vespers bell clanged, calling our congregation to the evening service. My mother and I were not going. Together we walked down the trail leading away from the camp into the gloom of the evergreen grove. The week we had spent at the camp had been awful for me. I felt like a foreigner, someone who didn't belong in that loving group of familiar church families. They had come to worship a God I was angry at, afraid of, and wanted to avoid.

"Why am I different? What makes me so anxious inside?" I asked my mother, choking on the words. I was ashamed of my behavior, but there was nothing else I could do.

"If God's so big, why did he make a mistake making me? Why am I so different?" Feeling the anger mounting within me as I kicked the dust in front of me into a small cloud, I added, "I guess Dad's gonna be mad at me for being this way."

"Nonsense, Jamie, he wants to understand," Mom said. "So do I. And, Jamie, so does God. If you're mad at God, then tell him—he can take it." Mom was crying, too, but softly. Whenever one of her children is in pain, she hurts.

A giant pine down the trail rose massively above its smaller neighbors, a god among its kind. Picking up a stone from the dark path, I threw it with all the force in my small body toward the tree. "Make me stop feeling this way! I don't like it, God!" I yelled. The rock fell short of its mark, but the point was made. I had told God exactly how I felt.

CHAPTER 4

New School, Old Grade

Dr. Carrie's diagnosis changed my life radically. Realizing that I wasn't so different, after all, made me feel better about myself. I wanted to work hard. I couldn't wait for the moment I would be called upon to stand up in class and spell—and be able to do it correctly. I didn't know then that it would take years of hard work before I could turn that dream into reality. That truth was brought home to me by a woman I will never forget.

My parents took Dr. Carrie's advice and immediately hired a professional tutor. I was informed that the most important things in my life would be my school lessons and my homework. I was not even to think about going out to play until my lessons and homework were completed—and completed to the satisfaction of Mrs. Blake, my tutor. I agreed. I didn't know what the word "discipline" really meant, but Mrs. Blake did. She was more than adequately equipped to pass on that understanding to a nine-year-old, hyperactive, learning-disabled little boy.

I was sitting in my room watching a brilliant, sun-filled

afternoon drift by, an afternoon that was perfect for playing with models and imaginary soldiers in the backyard or roaming the tide pools a few blocks from our home. It was not to be that sort of day, however, and I remember waiting with terror for the infamous green Chevy to turn our corner and unload its dread cargo. At the time, I thought it would be more appropriate if she flew in on a broomstick to harass me again and waste yet another of my afternoons.

Mrs. Blake was a woman in her sixties, lean and energetic, with steel-gray hair. She was a professional tutor with years of experience with cases like mine. She knew all the methods of instilling self-discipline and good study habits in children who otherwise would have a slim chance of making it through their schooling successfully. She understood, more than I, the need for strict observance of a tight schedule to compensate for my dyslexic habits.

She would enter my room and greet me, pulling from her voluminous teacher's bag books, pads, and large soft-lead pencils that dwarfed my hand. Our routine was set: reading, spelling, math, and finally physical tests to evaluate my coordination, balance, and motor ability. It was the reading I feared most, and she knew it. It was her habit to concentrate on the basics, to review and review again. We would select a paragraph in a reader for students far ahead of my reading ability and wade laboriously through it. Mrs. Blake would direct me to take one word at a time, and she would correct my pronunciation as I labored. It exhausted me to attempt even one of those monsters. Each time I finished I knew what to expect: "Now, James, let us concentrate on seeing the letters"— and with a terse nod of her head she would say the inevitable word: "Again!"

I remember one day when I completed an especially difficult paragraph after taking what seemed like an eternity to stumble through it. Mrs. Blake was in classic form and as usual instructed me to do it again. That time I refused, saying I couldn't. She corrected me: "You mean you 'won't,' not that you 'can't.' I will not tutor boys who 'won't'; therefore, you 'will.'"

I tried the last ploy I had. I cried in defiance. It got me nowhere. The order came again: "You will!" I obeyed. I finished the paragraph. Then I did it a third time and found myself being praised. It seemed that the witch wasn't so bad, after all. Before she left she told me she saw real improvement. All I saw was a real waste of a perfectly fine afternoon, but I didn't have much choice in the matter. I did want to be like my friends, and I had been told that if I worked with Mrs. Blake I would find school easier. One other thing drove me to continue with her, and that was the memory of too many failures before she came into my life. Even a nine-year-old knows when his spelling papers are improving, and mine were beginning to take an upward swing. At no time were my tutoring sessions easy, but the consistency of Mrs. Blake's methods and the constant discipline she provided were beginning to make sense. It was going to take much more time, however, before the rest of the world came to that same conclusion.

> WITH A TERSE NOD OF HER HEAD SHE WOULD SAY THE INEVITABLE WORD: "AGAIN!"

A tiny drop of glue dripped on the cardboard box that contained the last few pieces of the model awaiting assembly. My paint-smeared fingers gingerly gripped a landing gear I was attempting to connect to its struts beneath the airplane. The rain outside splattered my windows and trickled through my roof. Pans from the kitchen were placed around the floor to catch the streams of water that always appeared whenever we had a substantial shower. Dad had not yet finished his upstairs study or repaired the roof, and the cedar shingles stacked in the backyard would have to wait until he could squeeze some hours from his busy schedule. My hands dropped the plastic gear and smeared glue down the wing, and as I bent to pick up the part, I noticed Mrs. Blake's car outside, parked in its usual spot.

"This couldn't be Tuesday, not yet!" I exclaimed. "No, it's Monday, so why is her car here?" Putting down my model, I walked to the corner of my room and listened. Up in the living room I could hear voices. I sneaked into the kitchen and peered out the door. Mrs. Blake, my father, and my mother were gathered around the coffee table, discussing something. I crouched down next to a crack in the door and listened.

Sipping from her china cup, Mrs. Blake spoke: "If Dr. Carrie recommends it, then my vote goes that way, also. It will do the boy good to be ahead of his class for once."

My father added: "It certainly would be better to do it early in his education instead of waiting until high school. If it must be done, then now's the time. But he's the one who will have to live with the decision, so he'll have to make it."

"I want you both to know I think he could handle the next level up," Mrs. Blake said. "He has improved tremendously over the summer. In fact, there isn't much more I can do for him. All the same, I would feel better if he were to stay back." She sipped loudly as she drained her tea and my mom moved to refill the cup.

"If he does go back," Mom said, "I want him going to another school. It's embarrassing to be held back when all your friends are going ahead."

"Mrs. Evans, that seems to be inevitable," Mrs. Blake explained. "His present private school is closing next year, so he'll have to go elsewhere."

I closed the door and started downstairs. I had heard enough. So I was to change schools again—my fourth school in as many years. The thought hardly excited me, but what had they meant about "staying back"? It sounded hard, and I wasn't ready for another hard decision. It was enough to decide to be disciplined under my present workload without adding still one more decision.

Within minutes all three trooped into my room and sat down, my parents on the bed and Mrs. Blake in her usual chair. They told me they thought it would be wise if I stayed back in third grade that coming fall, instead of going on with my class to the next level. In any event, I would have to change schools, probably to a downtown public school that had special classes for students like me. I remembered Frankie Carlson, one of my second-grade classmates; he had to stay back a year. Suddenly I regretted giving him grief about being a second-grader when the rest of us were third-graders. Now it was my turn to take the ribbing. Watching the bowl on the floor near my feet fill up with drops of rainwater, I listened to the reasons why I should consider staying back.

> SO I WAS TO CHANGE SCHOOLS AGAIN—MY FOURTH SCHOOL IN AS MANY YEARS.

I didn't know anyone at the downtown school. If no one knew me, then how could they know I was in third grade for the second time? So I agreed to stay back a year and attend my new school.

Later, looking again into the box, I noticed a wheel gear left over. Somehow I had failed to attach it to the model plane's main assembly. Hoping it wouldn't matter, I continued with my project. No one was ever going to notice that I was short a few parts. Snapping the final gear with its painted rubber tire into place, I triumphantly placed the aircraft upright on the table. With horror I watched as it slowly listed to the left, finally canting crazily over its broken wheels. Frustrated, I referred to the instruction booklet wadded in the corner of my modeling bench. The illustrations didn't indicate which piece was missing or where it should have been installed. I would have to read the instructions. Groaning, I labored through the first sentence, becoming more confused than when I had picked up the booklet. I could make out the words if I went slowly, but conceptualizing the print into action was nearly impossible: The words didn't make sense. I had a better idea. Putting the instructions down, I picked up the model and the spare part, tested all the available holes that might accept it, and finally succeeded in attaching it to the wing just behind the main strut. Carefully, I bent the landing gear into the proper configuration and fastened it to the body. The plane rested sturdily on the desk, its gears now supported properly.

"Some help they were!" I grumbled. "The instructions must be written by someone who never built a model in his life."

Summer was approaching, and I expected a respite from my heavy study schedule. There were models to build and the beach was beckoning. I looked forward to skin diving with the boy across the street, my only close friend during those alienating hyperactive years; but the fight against dyslexia was not to cease during the summer months. I was told that if I wanted to retain all the wonderful gains I had made with Mrs. Blake and be well prepared for my new school in the fall, I would have to attend summer school.

San Diego was settled by Catholic missionaries, and to this day there are Catholic missions and schools dotting the coastal communities. It was in one of those sprawling institutions that I was enrolled for summer school, and every weekday morning my mother would drive me and a number of other children into town to attend half-day classes.

I remember the school as being very large, with Spanish-style buildings, huge gardens, fountains, chapels, playing fields, and, of great interest to me, statues. I had never seen statues of saints, and I was particularly fascinated by the figure of Saint Francis of Assisi surrounded by innumerable clay birds and small animals. He seemed a very kind man, and the expression on his face was comforting to me. But I was never allowed to stare for long. The habited nuns would hurry us from class to class with such energy that I thought surely they would trip over their flowing black robes. I had considered Mrs. Blake the sternest woman I ever met, but the cloistered sisters were giving her a run for the money. I never did understand how someone could look so much like an angel, yet spank so hard (which was allowed in those days). Nor had I escaped Mrs. Blake entirely. She made her usual appearances throughout the summer, toting her bag of books, pads, and enormous pencils.

While a young dyslexic is undergoing re-education, his parents are challenged almost as much as he is, but in different ways. They must see to it that he sticks to his rigid schedule, yet they must also keep up a constant level of encouragement and support. It isn't easy, and to this day I marvel at how well my parents were able to give me the most important things I needed. They continually reminded me of my goal. When I became frustrated by the endless repetition and effort involved in keeping up with my classwork, when I realized that life rarely offered me fun anymore, my parents would always point out that I was not being punished, nor was I dumb. Rather, I was a dyslexic who needed to work very hard. Many a time when I was depressed, my father would get out the chessboard and we would pore over it for hours. It was more than a game. It enabled me to prove to myself that I was bright.

As I repeated third grade in La Jolla Elementary School, my months of work began to pay off. My third-grade teacher, Mr. Russell, was a gentle man with a dark, pointed beard that made him look like a Spanish don. He was a very orderly person who prided himself on maintaining discipline. But the bulk of my work that year was done in a special room in a bungalow across the playground from the main school building. Once a day a number of us left Mr. Russell's class and went to the bungalow, where "special" students were taught in small groups by teachers who could give them the time and attention they required.

My group's instructor was a former bombardier in the Army Air Corps. He had seen combat in World War II and could tell the most wonderful stories about bombing raids and air combat. True to his former calling, he was also a stern disciplinarian who made Mr. Russell's orderliness seem mild by comparison. Yet there was a warmth about the man that his gruffness could not conceal. He loved oral recitation, and he could make reading and listening fun. I can still remember reading along in pure bliss with a recording of *Nikki, Wild Dog of the North*, losing myself completely in the exciting adventures. That was when I discovered that reading could be a pleasure. It was also the first time I ever excelled in the classroom.

Not all the "special" students had learning disabilities. In fact, I was in the minority. Most of the students who went to the bungalow every day had serious emotional and behavioral problems, and many had exceptionally low IQs. Consequently I had a decided edge over many of my classmates, and my experience under Mrs. Blake's discipline allowed me to feel comfortable under the ex-bombardier's regimen. The results were amazing. I began to excel in areas where I had always failed, and with accomplishments came the confidence to continue doing well. I was also enjoying the benefits of being a favored student, an honor I had always seen bestowed on others.

Unfortunately my lofty status was short-lived. I had done too well and was told I no longer qualified for extra help. I returned to full-time attendance in Mr. Russell's class, and after that I lapsed back into my former habits. Mr. Russell did his best to help, but there were thirty students in his class, compared to eight in the bungalow group, and he didn't have time to give me the close supervision I required. The second half of that school year was not nearly as successful, nor as enjoyable, as the beginning. I didn't know why, and I said nothing to my parents about my discomfort. But I had tasted success, however briefly, and I wanted to taste it again.

My father recalls walking into my room one evening during that period and finding me bent over my desk, working on a math assignment. He saw that I had been crying and had a hard time controlling my voice as I described what I was trying to do. I was working on long-division problems and failing miserably. Instead of spacing the problems over the paper, as I had been instructed to do, I had bunched them all together in the top left corner, which only added to my confusion as I attempted to make some sense out of the mess of figures. Dad remembers me clenching my teeth and plunging ahead, regardless of my tears. I don't remember that particular night, but there were many others like it, and I was determined not to give up, no matter how many hours I had to work.

It must have been very difficult for my parents to stand back and let me fight my battles, but that experience is essential for a learning-disabled child. As much as he or she needs help from others, that child is the one who has to make the major effort, and he or she must learn that lesson early in life. The worst thing in the world for me would have been having my parents pitch in and do what I had to do for myself.

> IT MUST HAVE BEEN VERY DIFFICULT FOR MY PARENTS TO STAND BACK AND LET ME FIGHT MY BATTLES.

My mother found special ways to help me through that difficult time. Since Mrs. Blake could not work with me every day, Mother saw to it that I did not forget that my fight was a daily business. Not being an iron-fisted disciplinarian, she found subtler ways of coaxing me to study. Like my ex-bombardier teacher, Mom showed me that reading could be fun. When I became frustrated looking at a page crammed with words that didn't make sense, ready to give up before I even began, my mother became creative. She cut a piece of cardboard to fit over the entire page of my reader, thus hiding the page of print. Then she would slide the card down, letting me take on a single line of words at a time. My eyes didn't skip from one line to another, as they did before, and eventually I could read to the bottom of the page—and don't think I didn't know I had accomplished something!

Sometimes Mom would make deals with me. If I would read a page, then she would read a page, and on and on until we finished a chapter. My mother was doing more than reviewing the basics of reading; she was encouraging me to try to read on my own. She also filled our house with Happy Hollisters and Hardy Boys books to help me discover that reading is an adventure. In many ways, being my mother was a full-time job, although I don't suppose my mother or anyone else ever thought of it in those terms. I realize now—and I hope she does—that she did her job well, and I'm grateful she found the time to give to it.

Eventually it became apparent that I could not yet hold my own in a large class. I completed third grade, but barely, and I faced the prospect of changing schools yet again. Much as I dreaded the prospect, something was happening inside me. It was as if Mrs. Blake had instilled a part of herself there because no matter how distasteful my assignment appeared to be, somehow I knew I would get through it. Slowly, perhaps. Beyond any doubt, with great difficulty. But . . . I . . . would . . . get . . . there.

In the meantime, another summer was on the way.

CHAPTER 5

Dying for Forgiveness

As I stepped off the small twin-engined island transport plane, I felt as if I had been hit in the face with a warm, damp washcloth. Storm clouds lazily drifted overhead, darkening the jungle canopy that surrounded the terminal of that West Indies paradise. Barbados was a wonderland to me. On the whitewashed walls of the Seawall Terminal on the south coast of the island I could see small chameleons and other lizards running about, perfect hunting targets for an eleven-year-old.

My father was on sabbatical and, needing a quiet place to vacation and study, had accepted an invitation to summer in a friend's quarters on the island. He and my mother were now accompanying a large group of teenagers and one eleven-year-old, heading toward a home on the less-populated side of the island to spend six weeks lying in the sun and enjoying the slow pace of the West Indies. My father planned to apply himself to scholarly pursuits in that unstudious atmosphere.

Our group consisted of fifteen people. When Dad had announced back in La Jolla that we would be heading south for the summer, my two brothers and sister had asked if they could bring their friends with us. Little did my parents realize how many friends were to be included: nine in all. The airport porter gave us a quizzical glance as my folks guided their youthful brigade to the nearest oversized (and soon to be overstuffed) taxi for our journey to the St. Lucia district of Barbados. I imagine the porter marveled at two parents being responsible for such a sizable brood, since the regulation blond hair and deep tan of La Jolla gave us all a similar appearance.

It was evening as we drove toward our new residence. I can remember the grand sugarcane plantations interspersed between the slopes of Mt. Hillaby, which rose gently at some points, and abruptly at others to eleven hundred feet above the surrounding ocean. Tiny, brightly painted cottages stood close to the roadside. They were the prefabricated dwellings of the island poor, the majority of the population who worked the sugar fields and mills that produced the island's primary exports of rum and molasses. The lush green of the area surprised me, accustomed as I was to California's arid terrain. Rich palms and breadfruit trees mingled with mahogany and flowering shrubs. Everywhere stray cane shoots sprouted across the hilly countryside. Occasionally we drove past cliffs overlooking long white beaches with mild surf that greatly disappointed my brothers. In the van, Tim groaned over his predicament. "How are we gonna surf those things? You can't even call them waves. Oh, man, no way, can't have six weeks of no surfing!" A stern glance from my father instantly silenced the griping as we charged on through the oncoming night.

Our headlamps caught two figures walking beside the road, carrying bundles on their heads. Shrieking, they both abandoned their loads and leaped into a ditch as our taxi driver expertly guided his machine within inches of them, quietly smirking to himself over his success in terrorizing the native population. We roared on through the night, swallowed up in a jungle darkness so deep that

I feared even our headlamps would be dimmed by it. The drone of the van and the warmth within sent me off into a bumpy sleep. I was awakened by a lurch as we pulled up to a building that looked like a warehouse surrounded by trees. I could dimly see a tin roof and glassless openings in the walls. This was the house.

The home was in a quiet section of the island, overlooking a bay that we normally had to ourselves except for a few cane workers. The house had once been a mill that processed cane into rum stock. Later it was converted to a slaughterhouse and was made into a private residence just after the war. A high wall surrounded the entire rear garden. An exquisitely dilapidated windmill jutted out from behind the house. It had been used to power the cane grinders in earlier times. On the other side of the house was a ruined pool that was the primary source of water before indoor piping was introduced. The pool was now filled with hideous toads. These toads secreted a poisonous fluid that was said to have killed a number of the island's dogs, who had been unfortunate enough to have made a meal of the small green monsters.

The bay was about two hundred yards from the house down a path often used by monkeys and other wildlife. Mongooses, rats, various brightly colored chameleons, and crabs of all sizes shared our dwelling space. I delighted in catching chameleons and watching them change color as I placed them on different surfaces. The cane workers' children taught me how to capture them with a noose made from a cane leaf. It was good to have time to play again.

On one of my return trips to the house from the bay where I spent most of the daylight hours, I felt a pain somewhere between my stomach and my heart, where my conscience lived. As I climbed the steep path the pain grew in intensity, covering my whole chest and filling my lungs, making it hard to breathe. I went into the bathroom to wash the sand from my skinny legs and feet, and the pain became almost unbearable. I began to cry. What could be causing such pressure within me on such a beautiful day? In my mind I began reliving all the stealing I had done during the past few years. The lies I had told rose before me with a ghostly vengeance, distorting the faces of those I had deceived into jeering monster masks. Something inside me was attempting to push out all the bad things I had done. Something wanted me to be clean inside and wanted me to stop thinking I was bad. Everything negative was coming to the surface.

I couldn't remain quiet any longer. I ran to the kitchen, where my mother was preparing our dinner. In tears I told her I had to talk to her, and after one look at my face she dropped everything and took me to her room. Immediately I began confessing to a myriad of petty thefts and lies. Then I proceeded to tell her my greater sins: pounding the next-door neighbor's son, cutting the wiring in a new house with a pair of my father's wire cutters—the list went on. As I confessed, the need to confess grew. It wasn't long before my father joined us. My parents listened in amazement as their youngest son revealed his life's secret wrongs. I was beside myself attempting to remember all the incidents I might have forgotten and wanted to get out of me. I was desperately looking for a way to release the guilt that had just exploded within me. My

> I FELT A PAIN SOMEWHERE BETWEEN MY STOMACH AND MY HEART, WHERE MY CONSCIENCE LIVED.

mother provided the key. She began telling me a story I had heard many times before but never really understood.

"Jamie, I want you to calm down and listen very carefully to me. I have a story to tell you that will make you feel better about the bad things you did. Now, Jamie, try to listen—Louie, give him a Kleenex to blow his nose."

Dad interjected: "Son, please try to listen to your mother. Here take this and wipe your eyes. Now look at her while she talks to you. It's all right, even big boys cry. Of course, it doesn't mean you're a sissy. Son, try to—Jamie, listen. That's better. Go ahead, Cokie."

"Jamie, you know how much we love you, right? Well, there's Someone Else who loves you more than we ever could. Do you know who that is?"

It was on that evening that my parents explained to me how Jesus died to take my guilt away from me. He didn't want his friends to feel anxious and guilty about the wrongs they had done. He wanted them to have an abundant life. All I had to do was confess what I had done wrong, and Jesus would lock it up far away where no one would ever see it again. I had heard those words a thousand times before, yet on that night they made sense to me for the first time. It was so simple, and I did my best to believe what they promised me.

> I WOULD TELL MYSELF THAT JESUS HAD PROMISED TO MAKE ME CLEAN AND GOOD.

Later that evening as the tree frogs made their usual racket outside, chirping like a flock of birds, and the cane beetles bumped against the walls in their blind flying, I went into battle. Each time the pain of guilt and anxiety would surface and I saw myself as a dummy and a bad boy, I would tell myself that Jesus had promised to make me clean and good. Perhaps it was simplistic, but it worked.

During the rest of my days in Barbados, Jesus and I became playmates. Whenever the feelings of guilt returned, telling me I was bad, my Friend wrestled with them. He took on what I was incapable of fighting: my poor self-esteem. Day by day my self-image improved, and as I began to believe that I could indeed be a good person, I set out to become one with a vengeance.

In Barbados, as in La Jolla, I had been a loner. But not anymore. I wanted to be with the people who loved me—constantly. As hard as my parents tried to supply my emotional needs, what they gave me during that traumatic time was never enough. I clung to them, just as I clung to Christ. Their love was not enough; I needed their presence. I felt Jesus with me every waking and sleeping moment, and I wanted my mother and father to be there, too. I began insisting that I sleep in my parents' room for the first few nights after I confessed all my past wrongs to them. Mom and Dad were very accommodating at first. My brother Dan was less understanding.

"Jamie, come here," Dan said, motioning me to follow him to his room. "I want to talk to you."

"Look," he began, once we were alone, "this is the folks' vacation, and I think it might be nice if we left them alone at night. I know it's scary sleeping all alone in the living room, but sometimes you have to consider other people."

Dan wasn't making any sense at all. "It's not as if I'm sleeping in the same bed with them," I said. "Anyway, they don't mind—they told me to sleep on the couch next to them." It took a not-too-subtle hint from Dad to remind me that my quarters in the living room were awaiting me and I had better get to them. I complied without argument. But my return to the living room did not stop me from bursting in on my parents at any hour of the night to admit another wrong I had just recalled as I was dozing off. It wasn't enough for me to confess my sins to Christ; I had to bring my parents in as intercessors. I must admit that I'm still embarrassed at all the times I made them listen to every minor infraction I had ever committed. But there was a fierce drive within me to be totally free of any guilt that might bring back the painful emotions I had felt that first day.

On the surface my reaction may appear typical of a fairly basic "conversion to the faith": a young boy realized his errors and desired an intimate relationship with Jesus Christ as a friend and as one who would relieve him of the guilt load he had been carrying. This explanation satisfied both my parents and me at the time. Only recently have I begun to understand what really happened. A simplistic explanation could not account for the deep emotional conflicts I faced during the coming years. After I accepted Christ, I became a super-disciplined person who could not dare to trespass in the slightest way. My stealing, lying, and abusive behavior ceased because my new conscience could not tolerate even a fraction of guilt-producing wrong. This was not a love of what is good, which Christ truly is, but rather a fear of the bad. I saw the world in terms of black and white, and feared the dark foe who was attempting to tell me I was bad. Every now and then, he got the better of me.

My oldest brother, Dan, was a disciplined man with a talent for designing and shaping surfboards. Eighteen months older than my next brother, Tim, Dan organized and ran the Evans Surf Shop, specializing in custom-made boards constructed to match the client's body type

and surfing ability. It wasn't long before Evans boards
were popular items on the beaches of San Diego. I can
still recall Dan's yelling at the less disciplined but more
artistic Tim to "get his act together and finish the board"
that Dan had shaped. It was Tim's responsibility to put
the coats of fiberglass and coloring over the Styrofoam
blanks that Dan cut into high-speed, wave-cutting craft.
By nature Tim was a quiet, brilliant, sensitive person who
could play classical guitar as well as he could ride the
waves. He had the best brains in the family, while Dan
had the dedicated work habits that enabled the surf shop
to meet its commitments.

My brothers were a familiar pair on the La Jolla
beaches, well-known for their prowess on the waves. Both
were powerfully built, and with their blond hair, tan skin,
and custom boards, they were quite a breathtaking sight
as they won one surfing contest after another against
some of southern California's best competitors. It was
common for them to leave our house at six in the morning, rev up the old Taunus car, and head for the beach
to get into the surf before school. They would often return home at dusk after long hours on the beach, their
ears full of sand, their dripping wetsuits draped over
shoulders pumped up and swollen from the strain of paddling out through the driving surf and dodging oncoming
buddies as they made their way to their takeoff point.
Dinner was frequently held up because a last-minute set
of very surfable waves happened to appear on the horizon
as Dan and Tim were leaving for home.

Since I was still a child and had not developed the
body strength required for surfing, I didn't accompany my
brothers. After school I stayed at home, working with my
battery of tutors who helped me wage war against my
learning disability. As I look back now, I cannot remember one occasion, from the age of eight to thirteen, when
my brothers and I did anything together, except our an-

nual family vacation. I was less-than-desirable company for them, but the difference in our ages and interests also separated us. Whatever the cause, I took it personally. I felt my brothers had rejected me.

Having perceived myself as bad and dumb at an early age, I looked for opportunities to confirm that low opinion of myself. I had always been told by my mother, "Jamie, love is an action, not just a word. We do love." That definition would ring in my brain as I watched my brothers troop off together, leaving me at home to entertain myself. If Mom was right and we "do love," then my being alone most of the time meant something. My negative self-image was quick to seize upon the situation as proof that "if they don't spend time with you, and they don't talk to you, then they *don't* love you . . . and we all know whose fault that is!" This inner animosity kept repeating to me that "no time" meant "no love," and it was all my fault.

One afternoon, noticing my brothers' car missing from the driveway, I crept into the surf shop. My brothers had gone to pick up more supplies and grab a quick surf before dark. I was alone. As I stepped into the shaping room, the scent of resin and catalyst attacked my nose, making me a little dizzy. The place reeked of the fumes coming from the glassing room. The floor was littered with drippings of the colorful mix that sheathed the soft Styrofoam blank, giving it rigidity and beauty. A rack in front of me cradled a freshly shaped six-foot-long blank

> HAVING PERCEIVED MYSELF AS BAD AND DUMB AT AN EARLY AGE, I LOOKED FOR OPPORTUNITIES TO CONFIRM THAT LOW OPINION OF MYSELF.

awaiting its outer skin of resin. Tim hadn't gotten around to glassing it yet, which wasn't uncommon. Dan would be pushing him to make their deadline.

The white of the blank beckoned to me. I wanted to touch it but hesitated, remembering Dan's stern warnings: "Jamie, don't let me catch you fooling with our boards! Keep your hands off the blanks, especially the freshly shaped ones. They're really easy to dent. Do I make myself clear?"

But Dan wasn't around to enforce his rule. Something inside me told me to touch the blank; I wouldn't hurt it. Checking the driveway again, I saw no one. I had my chance. Running my dirty hand over the soft blank, I marveled at how smoothly Dan had formed it with his planer. He was getting to be a master at his craft. Suddenly an urge seized me. I pressed my thumb into one of the carefully sanded rails along the side of the board. The soft foam yielded to my pressure and dented slightly. A strange joy filled me, and I repeated my action on the opposite side. Slipping out of the shop entrance, I tiptoed away, glancing back long enough to catch sight of the white blank resting on its rack, my two thumbprints clearly visible on the neatly sanded rails.

It wasn't long before I learned that it wasn't a good idea to express my anger in that way. My brothers helped me reach that conclusion. But I kept the anger inside me and took it with me to Barbados. There it turned on me; there in that island paradise it attacked me with all the years of self-doubt, the endless classroom failures, and the rejection of my peers.

Yet, when Jesus took control of my young life during that family vacation he began a healing process that would go on for years. Eventually he would resolve every trace of anger and self-doubt. He would employ some of the best specialists available, he would bring much prayer and discipline into my life, he would inspire love and patient care from parents and future friends. All these resources would be used by my Lord to heal the scarring in my life. Christ had committed himself to my rebuilding and renewal, and he dug down into my inner being to remove every cancerous cell of self-hate and anger.

CHAPTER 6

I Discover the Benefits of Control

The morning sun shone through a partly shuttered window. An old clock ticked away nearby and rang off fifteen-minute increments with its ancient bell. I sat examining a dust particle's flight as it lazily floated through the light that streamed onto the floor before my feet. With a gentle swipe of my hand, I sent it toward the ceiling, where it suddenly vanished as it slipped from the sun's rays.

The library in which I waited was small, no more than ten feet by twelve. It was located in the front of the Evans School of La Jolla (no relation to my family), a private school that emphasized controlled classes and individual attention for the "special student." I wasn't sure what a "special student" was, but I had an idea that I qualified.

The dust speck reappeared in the light about knee level and caught my attention again. I was so engrossed in its flight pattern that I didn't notice the door behind me opening. A gray-haired woman in her late forties or early fifties entered. She stood no more than five feet two, well below my eleven-year-old, five-foot-ten-inch frame, yet her presence commanded respect. Her pursed lips gave the distinct impression that she would tolerate no nonsense. I was jolted from my observations of the dust speck by her greeting.

"Young man, I am Mrs. Baird. My daughter Gale will administer the entrance examination to you," she said. Before I could extend my hand, she turned and led me into a side classroom that at one time had been a living room in the converted house. Realizing that there was very little I could do to put off the inevitable, I dropped my hand and followed obediently.

Mrs. Baird was not given to small talk. I was hoping for better luck with her daughter—anything to avoid another test. I hated entrance exams. It seemed I was always changing schools, and the exams were the signal that I was about to be thrust into a new world all over again. This was my fifth school in as many years, and I was tired of changing friends.

Gale Baird greeted me with a smile and a friendly handshake. She was a pretty twenty-two-year-old fresh out of college. She was beginning her teaching career alongside her mother and was responsible for testing prospective students. She ushered me to a seat, handed me a battery of tests, and told me to begin immediately. With a groan I dove into the mass of papers and answer sheets, occasionally glancing up at the attentive Gale, hoping for some sign of sympathy. I got none and had to be content with frequent trips to the pencil sharpener for relief.

With a sigh of finality I dotted the last *i* and closed the booklet. I have never bothered to reread tests. I handed the booklet to Gale, hoping for a speedy getaway, but she gave it back to me without even opening it. "Reread it and check your spelling before you hand it in," she ordered firmly. *Betrayed! I had been betrayed!* Her kind face and young age had promised me a girl who would let an eleven-year-old relax, and now she was getting strict. With a frown meant to be noticed, I headed back to my desk muttering, "Yes, ma'am!"

I could see it coming: if I got into the Evans School, I could say good-bye to the canyon and my models for the rest of the year. I could smell homework coming my way.

Squirming, I opened the booklet and read what I had written. I could hardly sit still. I hated to read, let alone reread what I had just written. It bored me. I never found anything wrong with what I had written, anyway, although I was sure Mrs. Baird would find plenty. My impatience increased, but I endured it, knowing that I'd pay if I didn't correct my work. These people meant business.

> I COULD SMELL HOMEWORK COMING MY WAY.

After I handed in the test, I was escorted by the two women to the back seat of a green MG hatchback. Mother and daughter buckled into the front seat and prepared to drive me home. At the wheel Mrs. Baird was a terror. We zipped through the hills of La Jolla at speeds befitting my seventeen-year-old brother, not a fifty-year-old headmistress. As I watched the scenery whiz by the rear window, I suspected that my life was about to be changed by still more discipline.

Our family had recently returned from Barbados, and my parents and I had decided that it was time for me to be enrolled in a school with small classrooms. The Evans School seemed to meet my needs perfectly, but now I was beginning to regret my decision to try it. As I watched the last days of summer roll past, and the Santa Ana winds arrived bringing temperatures of 95 degrees only days before school opened, I was entering a state of anxiety. I was in good company. In my classroom on the first day of school were twelve uniformed fifth-graders, each one displaying some form of fear at the prospect of beginning a year of individual attention.

Like the other boys in my class, I wore gray slacks, a blue short-sleeved, button-down shirt, a clip-on striped tie, and hard shoes polished shiny black. The girls wore red-and-blue jumpers, white knee socks, and saddle shoes. The uniforms were the outward expression of the school's educational philosophy: discipline and order, the basics stressed with particular care given to affirming a student at every possible opportunity.

The Evans School was attempting to instill academic pride within its flock and was utilizing discipline to this end. As a dyslexic, I needed sizable portions of both: discipline to develop the work habits I would need to compensate for my disability, and pride in my newfound accomplishments to counteract the negative self-image caused by my past failures. Failure was not allowed at the Evans School; there was simply too much encouragement built into the curriculum for that to happen.

Mrs. McCarthy, our fifth-grade teacher, was well into her sixties, and her steel-gray hair and makeup bespoke a person who adhered to fashions long since gone. She, too, was a no-nonsense woman and from the beginning let it be known that we were expected to meet very high standards of behavior. Talking out of turn, teasing one another, throwing or spitting objects, pulling hair, cheating—all were intolerable.

At Evans the term "special student" included high achievers as well as those with learning disabilities: it meant anyone who might benefit from small classes and close supervision. At first I was terrified at the thought of being the slowest student in my class, but that never happened. The goals set by the more able students encouraged the rest of us to try to reach them, and amazingly some of us did. A few of the learning-disabled kids worked their way up to the level of the high achievers in some subjects, and I don't think that would have been possible in a class where everyone learned slowly.

We were taught in carefully proctored small groups designed to accelerate the able and encourage the slow. Gradually I advanced to an accelerated reading group, and for the first time in my life I was in the top percentile of my class. Some of the children with learning disabilities had more serious problems than mine, and I should have been able to do better than they—but to compete with some of the good grade-getters? To begin accumulating gold stars and all kinds of prizes for good work? That was beyond any of the fantasies I had had since I was diagnosed. I was beginning to see that discipline and control were the keys to success for me, and I wondered how many more doors might open if I began using discipline and control more conscientiously.

A red, manicured fingernail tapped on my desk, pointing to the math problem I had just finished. Mrs. McCarthy, standing over me, had been watching my long division and apparently had found an error. It wasn't unusual for her to find mistakes only moments after I made them. She was continually cruising the class, keeping a sharp eye on the slower and more error-prone students. Tapping her index finger on my paper again, she asked, "Where do you see a mistake, Jamie? There's a careless error in plain sight."

I had failed to reread my math work that day. Sometimes I just didn't have the patience to go to the extra trouble. Reading back over it, I found the error. As usual, it was a reversal: I had interchanged a six for a nine, which made all the difference in my denominator.

Sheepishly I erased the number and replaced it with the correct one. Hoping for approval, I looked up to the woman hovering over me. She still wasn't satisfied; her expression told me there was more to correct. A tinge of impatience shot through me, making me squirm in my chair, but I had to check once more. I found that I had allowed one of my columns to wander, confusing my subtraction. That was a messy mistake, and I knew I was in trouble. Reversals Mrs. McCarthy could forgive, but not messiness. Her silence was punishing as she walked from my area and continued her scan of the rest of the class. I figured she'd be back with a lecture on neatness, but first she'd let me stew for a while. She was a pro.

Mrs. McCarthy was also a very wise person. She watched her twelve students like a mothering hawk, careful to compliment any achievement, no matter how small, and continually correcting any sign of negative study habits. Before I enrolled in the Evans School, I was often frustrated to tears by failure in math. The numbers always got impossibly rearranged by my malfunctioning brain, making most of my answers incorrect. For me to read an instruction sheet explaining the theory behind an exercise and then apply that theory was nearly impossible. It was far better for me to be told verbally how a theory worked and then to take that concept and put it to work.

The written page is a dyslexic's nightmare, and our culture's traditional use of writing to convey knowledge puts the dyslexic at a terrible disadvantage. Mrs. McCarthy understood this problem. Steadily, patiently, boosting me whenever I earned it in the slightest, she would explain theory to me verbally, staying with me until she was convinced I understood how to connect the idea with the necessary action or solution, as the case was in math. She combined her verbal explanation with the instructions I was reading until they made sense to me, and once that happened I could go on from there.

Soon I was mastering long and short division, times tables and multiplication, and as I became more competent, much of my earlier frustration began to fade. Even though I was still reversing numbers, I was actually enjoying math. There again Mrs. McCarthy came to the rescue. She would force me to check and recheck my work. Then she would order me to read backward what I had jotted down, which removed any sensible meaning from the numbers or words before me and focused all my energies on the correctness of spelling and order. My hyperactivity fought her every inch of the way. It was painfully difficult for me to sit still long enough to correct my work, yet her eagle eye never left me until I faithfully accomplished what she assigned. Between my terror of her punishment and her sheer patience, we dealt some severe blows to hyperactivity, and as my attention span rose so did my grades.

OUR CULTURE'S TRADITIONAL USE OF WRITING TO CONVEY KNOWLEDGE PUTS THE DYSLEXIC AT A TERRIBLE DISADVANTAGE.

I was learning how to control my academic environment, trying with everything in me to hold off failure and rejection. The more I achieved, the more secure I felt. But I paid a price for that radical reversal of my past habits. I became more easily frustrated and anxious. After a long day under the iron hand of Mrs. McCarthy, I had to force myself to sit down and complete hours of assigned homework. The Evans School faculty put a great deal of emphasis on homework because they believed that education is a constant process that goes beyond the classroom. In my case it left hardly any time for my beloved canyons or any other recreation. I didn't object. In fact, I became frantic if I thought I wouldn't complete my work for the next class day. Through that work I was earning the first affirmation I had received outside my home and I was not going to give it up.

> I WAS LEARNING HOW TO CONTROL MY ACADEMIC ENVIRONMENT, TRYING WITH EVERYTHING IN ME TO HOLD OFF FAILURE AND REJECTION.

On a winter weekend my parents decided to truck us all off in a camper to the San Gabriel Mountains. As we were returning from the rare outing, a horrible dread came over me. *What if I get home too late to finish my homework?* I thought. *What if I have to go into class unprepared? Will Mrs. McCarthy punish me?*

The fear spread and my anxiety would not quit until I raced back into the house ahead of my suitcase-lugging brothers and dove into my books. I could not allow myself to lose even a day's control of my schoolwork and the rewards it brought me. I could not allow dyslexia to get the upper hand again. I was in a struggle for my future.

As the struggle became more and more a part of my life and as I began to use control as a weapon, my anxiety increased. I was expending huge amounts of emotional energy and beginning to feel the consequences. My stuttering hit an all-time high, and that was a danger signal. Too much energy was going out with too little rest coming in.

My sixth-grade teacher at the Evans School was a tall,

lean athletic woman who was also responsible for planning the school sports program that year. Usually we were bused off to the community center, which offered large concrete playing fields and one track. Being naturally given to running, our teacher decided we should follow her example.

On the first day of spring she announced that we would be tested for our endurance in long-distance running, and if we wanted to be prepared we had better get jogging! We were quite a sight that day: forty children clad in blue jeans and tennis shoes, slogging around the track, raising clouds of dust in the La Jolla heat. For most of the students it inspired little joy, and complaints were the rule. But for a few, running became a pleasure. I was surprised at the way I felt after the first half-mile, when all the kinks had worked themselves out and lunch had settled. There was an ease about setting a pace and holding to it just behind some of the bigger sixth-graders. Later, in the classroom, my hyperactivity was somewhat reduced and my concentration improved. At the time I didn't tie the running and the concentration together, but unknowingly I had been given the solution to my overabundance of energy. Long-distance running was about to ease much of the tension that came from my attempts to control my hyperactivity through mental discipline. It even reduced my stuttering.

During my first year in the Evans School the Barbados experience remained in the back of my mind. I was reading the Bible and praying daily. My faith was maturing as I grew closer to Christ, and my stealing and lying had come to an end. But with the beginning of my second year, I experienced a strange reaction that to this day disturbs me. I began to recall how I behaved in Barbados, admitting all my wrongs, and I was ashamed of losing control of my emotions. It was my low self-image resurfacing, and I was almost overwhelmed by a barrage of guilt. I felt the same pain I had felt in Barbados—it flushed across the back of my head, my appetite tumbled; at times the tension was so great that I even threw up. I didn't understand what was happening within me or why, but I couldn't tell anybody. I was afraid I would bring more shame and guilt down on myself.

Though I still struggled, the Evans School began to win out over my old guilt feelings from Barbados. By the end of my second year I was a class leader, and I had friends, good friends. I was learning how to play, how to share another person's interests, and my sense of unworthiness was beginning to fade. For the first time I had a stable group of friends. With the five other boys in my class I relished the prospect of going to seventh grade at a small nearby private boys' school that had recently merged with a much larger girls' school. The ratio of girls to boys would be three hundred to thirty. We were a bit young to appreciate what a ten-to-one ratio could mean for a budding seventh-grader's social life, but we sensed that something exciting was about to happen.

CHAPTER 7

Running, Running

There were girls everywhere! Their plaid uniforms and white starched collars made them all appear the same from a distance, and I could not believe that for every one of us boys there were ten girls. My two friends and I stuck together as we made our way to the chapel for the opening-day convocation. Our egocentric adolescent minds told us that every pair of female eyes was fixed upon us, three lone males attempting not to be conspicuous in a sea of giggling females ranging from seventh through twelfth grade.

For the older boys in our newly merged school this was the stuff dreams were made of. Here were three hundred of the most tanned and best-educated girls in La Jolla. Having recently come from an all-male academy, they were delighted immeasurably. But for myself and my two fellow seventh-graders, it was a nightmare. As we sat in the Bishop's School chapel with its high ceilings, barrel vaults, and Spanish accents, we were frantically trying to find a quick means of escape, being too young to appreciate our great fortune.

In the Evans School the classes were small and everyone knew everyone else. The sixth-graders ruled the lower classes with all the authority befitting their rank. I had no idea it could be so uncomfortable starting all over again—as a very little frog in a very big pond.

The last of the seniors paraded into the chapel and took their seats. The headmaster, Mr. Perkins, opened the ceremony from a podium in front of us, but before I could catch what he was saying, I felt a jab in my ribs that nearly sent me tumbling from my seat. One of my companions had spotted a particularly cute seventh-grader opposite us and had managed to get a smile out of her. He was now attempting to repeat the feat with me looking on. It seemed that he wasn't as shy as I had thought, which made me feel all the more awkward at my own social backwardness. I focused my gaze on the headmaster more out of embarrassment than real interest. He was a man in his forties, with a wisp of gray in his full head of hair and an athletic frame. He reminded me of my father: authoritative and gifted with a presence.

HERE WAS A NEW WORLD FULL OF GIRLS AND BOYS WHO SEEMED FAR AHEAD OF ME SOCIALLY.

I liked him immediately but also feared him. He concluded his talk by saying that much would be expected of us in the coming year, and if we were to glean the full measure that Bishop's had to offer, we had better apply ourselves to our tasks with all our vigor.

Academics was the last thing on my mind, however. Here was a new world full of girls and boys who seemed far ahead of me socially. I was determined not to be left behind like some awkward kid who couldn't handle himself in a crowd. If the boy beside me could enjoy the abundance of females, then so could I. And with that conviction planted firmly in my mind, I trooped with my friends out of the chapel to begin my first day of classes.

That conviction was a mistake. No one can serve two masters and be successful with both. My academic gains at the Evans School came largely from a single-minded devotion to my studies in and out of class. As a new seventh-grader, I was fascinated by the social scene, which was a great distraction from my studies. For a typical seventh-grader, adapting to the social changes of junior high is a major part of education. But I was not a typical seventh-grader. My learning disability was still a force to be reckoned with. It demanded my undivided attention if I was to continue to climb out of its clutches.

I sat there, humiliated. The paper in front of me was crisscrossed with red ink. The C-minus in bold lettering on the front baffled me. I looked at my Latin teacher in disbelief. A few months earlier I had received the Latin prize from the Evans School. Now I was getting the lowest grade in my Latin I class. What was happening to me?

"Jamie, would you like to meet after class and discuss your grade?" she asked.

I nodded in agreement as I returned to my seat, choking on the lump in my throat, and turned to the window to hide the tears that ran down my face. Hadn't it been only three weeks ago that she had asked me if I had wanted to be advanced to the Latin II class after she had looked at my Evans School transcripts? And now I was close to failing Latin I! I was the only boy in the small class, which didn't help matters much. As other students returned from receiving their papers, I stared out the window. The morning fog drifted across the quad lawn, camouflaging the Spanish arches and tiled roof of the dorm across from my class. One moment I would see a distant tree and bench. The next moment, all would be swallowed up in a white blur.

I wanted to run into that blur and be swallowed up, to hide from the paper and the teacher before me that told me I needed still more help, that I wasn't making the grade. From deep down inside, an old voice haunted me, struggling up to my brain: *Dummy, big dummy! What else did you expect, stupid? You know you're stupid. Look at the papers around you. You've got the lowest grade in the class—dummy!* With an effort I pushed the voice back to where it had come from and turned my attention to the lesson on the board. I didn't feel very good.

"Miss Larson, when you explain it, I can do it, but that primer confuses me and I—"

"Jamie, you simply must concentrate on your assignments. There is no reason why I should explain every detail about our homework assignment when it's written in plain English before you," she prodded.

"But I do concentrate, and—"

"Now, not another word, young man. Do as you're told, and concentrate. You must apply yourself more. You are dismissed." She excused me with a wave of her hand.

Concentrate. How could I concentrate when I didn't understand what I was supposed to be concentrating on? Written instructions baffled me. If I could just get her to explain the exercises in detail and try a couple with me, the way they used to do in the Evans School, I might have a chance, but under the Bishop's School system I was lost. The frustration mounted, and again I was forced to choke back that lump in my throat. The Bishop's School was designed for self-motivated, bright students, enabling them to soar beyond any public school education offered in the area. But, as a dyslexic, I needed more personal time with a teacher who would carefully explain what I had missed in my reading. By seventh grade, most students were more than capable of reading instructions and following them on their own. Yet that was my weak area, and I was having a hard time explaining it to my teachers. I could read and reread the instructions and still make a mess of my assignment because of my perceptual difficulties.

I could taste the frustration with its telltale anger and that lump in my throat. With the repeated low grades in my classes came a change in my work habits. The drive I had developed over the two years at Evans was waning and my disciplined attitude toward homework weakened.

Science class was a different experience. We met in a large, windowless classroom that looked more like a box than a room. I was fascinated by the numerous gas and water spigots protruding from the black-topped tables that lined the room. Each spigot was color coded to identify the gas it spewed. In the nooks and crannies of the classroom were old instruments that measured and weighed compounds, and the sparkle of Pyrex glassware was everywhere. Our teacher was a bespectacled young man with a bushy beard and keen eyes. He had a way of making class exciting and would carefully explain what we were reading. When books and lectures couldn't get a point across, he would use film and demonstrations. Some might have accused him of oversimplifying his subject, but his painstaking explanations and illustrations were perfect for me. What confused me in the printed matter was made clear in class. I found myself doing well in his course and spending a great deal more time preparing for it than for the courses in which I was doing poorly and needed the most work. But science class was an exception. In the others my grades fell radically, as I went from an A average at Evans to a C or below at Bishop's.

There is no such thing as stasis when one is fighting a disability. When I was not building good study habits, then I was losing them. The effort to maintain discipline is a conscious choice. Although I had done well at the Evans School, I could not afford to live off the spoils of my past achievements. New disciplines and work habits had to be developed to continue the momentum I had attained. This I had failed to do, however, and my grades and self-esteem suffered.

During this setback my father came home with an announcement that changed the lives of all of us.

A small gray-and-white speckled lizard dashed from his rocky perch across the sandstone ledge and paused, panting slightly, before my feet. With a flick of his tail he was gone over the edge of the escarpment, scurrying down into the bushes below. Aside from the pebbles that tumbled after him and the cars on the highway below, all was quiet in my canyon. I crouched down and put my face near a sandstone cleft, following the trail of a red ant carrying his unfortunate prey off to his subterranean vault. The black ant held firmly in the red ant's jaws wriggled fruitlessly, trying to get away.

Carefully, I took a sage branch and flicked the red ant from behind. Dropping his prey he turned, jaws open, to defend himself, and the tiny black ant raced away while the red ant dueled with my stick. Feeling a prick on my leg, I found a cousin of the red ant biting hard through my blue jeans. I stood and brushed the attacker off and continued down the well-worn trail. Overhead, sage bushes camouflaged my movements as I neared the eucalyptus grove along the dry streambed.

I climbed up the two-by-fours nailed to the tree and reached the first level of the old fort built by previous generations of canyon users. I settled back against a familiar branch and felt sick. I thought back to the scene in the family room a half hour earlier.

We had all gathered there. Tim was dripping wet, his wetsuit slung over the stool in the kitchen. Apparently there had been a good set of waves at the last minute, which explained his tardiness. Andie and I, fresh from school, were still in our uniforms. Mom and Dad sat on the couch, looking serious. Something was happening. We had been summoned by Dad and it was he who began.

"Kids, my work here in La Jolla is almost finished," he said. "The church has a mature staff, there's plenty of lay support, so I've done all I can here. Though it would be nice to stay and enjoy the benefits of our work, I feel this might be the time God is telling us to move on to a new challenge."

Andie and Tim exchanged worried glances. Where was Dad planning to move us? Tim was a senior in high school. I could understand why he didn't want to be uprooted only months before his graduation. Andie, a junior at Bishop's, had similar feelings. Dan had left the year before for college at Santa Barbara, so he wasn't affected.

"I've received a call to the National Presbyterian Church in Washington, D.C., and I want to know how you feel about it," Dad said. A shock ran through my spine. I had never been east. I could only guess what it was like, and I was terrified. I was only beginning to feel socially comfortable at Bishop's. Would I be leaving again?

"If Dad accepts the call, we'll be moving sometime in late January or early February," Mom added. My stomach took a turn. That meant I'd be going into a new school in the middle of the year. It was hard enough to get involved in a school as a new student, but in the middle of the year I'd stand out like a sore thumb. Things were rapidly going from bad to worse.

My father did accept the call, and it was quickly decided that Tim would remain in La Jolla to finish high
school. Andie and I had a decision to make. We both
had been offered accommodations in the dorms at
Bishop's, so if we chose, we could stay and continue our
education. One look at Mom's face, though, and Andie
knew what her decision was going to be. It would have
hurt Mom terribly to be separated from all her flock so
suddenly. Andie decided to go to D.C., and I followed
suit. Though I hated to leave La Jolla, I dreaded even
more being separated from my parents. There was a
rightness about the decision, too: I knew I was supposed to go.

I didn't know anyone in Washington, D.C. I hated the
idea of starting a new school in the middle of winter. I
was tired of changing schools and wanted to settle down
where I was. *Maybe I could get my grades up,* I thought.
My homework assignments flashed across my mind. I still
hadn't finished them, but since I wasn't going to be
around much longer, I dismissed the thought, something
I never would have done at the Evans School. It seemed
like a long time ago when I used to rush home and finish
my homework before I went outside.

I tried to visualize what Washington, D.C., was like,
where I would go to school, and whom I would befriend.
The prospects depressed me and thinking about homework made me feel frustrated and pressured. I climbed
down the tree to the underground fort at its base. Remembering the last time I had ventured into it to find
that a rattlesnake had gotten there before me, and not
wishing to compound my worries by a similar encounter,
I avoided the fort and headed back home. The sun was
setting over the Pacific as a layer of fog rolled in. I wondered if D.C. had any beaches and whether I would be
able to get lost in the fog there as easily as I did in La
Jolla. Nothing was better than running through my can-

yon in a heavy fog. In that kind of weather I could create worlds all my own where no one could find me.

I stood at the window of my homeroom in my new junior high, watching two janitors raise the Maryland state flag in the gray early morning. A light snow was falling and the nearby street lights were just flickering off. Behind me the classroom was filling as my fellow seventh-graders checked in. I ached inside. I wanted to be one of those janitors, or even the bus driver now pulling out of the drive after his last delivery—anyone, anywhere but who I was. As the flag ascended and the two men tied off the connecting rope, I felt my stomach do a familiar burn.

The first-period bell rang, and I knew that gym class was just around the corner. I tried not to look too anxious as I pushed through the double doors to the locker room, which was filled with classmates, the floor strewn with clothes and shoes. As I headed for my locker, thinking that this time I would make it without trouble, a hand grabbed my arm and threw me against the wall. Another hand clenched into a fist jabbed into my stomach while my classmates looked on. A second fist crashed into my shoulder. Blinded with anger and fear, I lashed out with all the pent-up anxiety that had been building that morning. My fist found its mark on the chin of one of my attackers, and as he reeled back his buddy blindsided me against the far wall. Both smirking, they strutted off to their lockers, conveniently located next to mine.

I was the new boy in class and was receiving "the welcome" to impress upon me who were the bosses of our grade. I watched my first attacker begin to change. I was baffled because he had such a bulging wallet stuffed with fives and tens, and he made the rounds before class collecting what he called "orders." Later I learned that, aside from being a first-rate bully, he also was one of the many go-betweens who passed drugs from the high school dealers to the seventh-grade customers. My second attacker was one of his most frequent customers, a boy who was sometimes so high before school that he could hardly pronounce his name correctly at roll call. I had never really hated anyone before, but I was learning how to hate those two very quickly. My size had made me a potential rival to them and they took a special interest in teaching me my place.

It seemed as if years had passed since we had left La Jolla one rainy January day. Remembering my days at Bishop's with its whitewashed, clean Spanish architecture and year-round blooming gardens, I found it difficult to be thankful for my new school. I hated it, and I hated the two boys who shared locker space with me. I had never been a fighter, but now I was fighting almost weekly just to make it around the halls. The school's stark, carpetless floors and institutional surroundings did little to increase my appreciation for the place. Had I actually been here for two weeks? Why did we have to leave La Jolla? I glared at the two boys dressed in gym shorts beside me. They had done their best to make my first two weeks in school a hell, and I wanted to get back at them for it. At night I would feel guilty for hating them and would ask for forgiveness in my prayers, trying my best to follow my Lord's commandment to pray for my enemies. But during the day my guilt would quickly turn to anger and hatred as I anticipated them hiding around corners or waiting for me in the locker room.

> **AS I HEADED FOR MY LOCKER, A HAND GRABBED MY ARM AND THREW ME AGAINST THE WALL.**

In class I faced a situation quite the opposite of what I had expected. Just a few weeks earlier, at Bishop's, I had been on the verge of failing; now I was forging ahead, completing the work with little trouble and making grades that topped those made during my best days at the Evans School. It wasn't that I worked harder at my new school—actually I was doing less homework than before—but its standards were far below those of Bishop's. Kids literally had to try to fail, and most breezed through with little or no work outside the classroom.

Strangely, my academic successes did little to make me like the school. After Bishop's, even with low grades, and the success at Evans School, I had been conditioned to expect much more from a school than my new school could offer. I began to see school as a place to be avoided. I dreaded leaving my house in the morning to set off for the bus stop. I was jealous of my sister, who somehow had been able to enroll in the National Cathedral School for Girls, the best private girls' school in the city, and she could do nothing but sing its praises when she returned home each evening. I, too, had tried to get into the area's private schools, but there was no room in any of them.

I longed to return to La Jolla. I would gladly have sacrificed my As here for C-minuses at Bishop's, if only I could get away from those two kids who seemed too tough to be real, who were constantly bragging about their latest drug use, and who had a fetish for fighting.

At Bishop's I had allowed many of my disciplined habits to slip, and my grades had shown it. In my new school I was allowed to let those habits slip even farther, and still I received As. I was beginning to find classes boring and did less and less in the way of work. For a learning-disabled child, motivation is a primary weapon in the battle. With it he or she can develop the discipline to compensate for the disability. I was quickly losing what little motivation I had left. If it hadn't been for a sign that I noticed on the bulletin board one day, I might have lost my battle altogether.

Our coach had posted a sign-up sheet for the track team, and I found myself with fifty other seventh-through ninth-graders, trooping off to our first organizational meeting. The combination of my father's track stories and the running at Evans had convinced me that this was something worth looking into. We began meeting every day in the locker room after school to suit up for our practice. Neither of my enemies had bothered to sign up for such a disciplined sport, and for two hours I found myself unmolested, free to run and make friends without worrying about who was sneaking up behind me. It was my first really enjoyable experience at the school.

> YET FOR ALL THE HARD WORK AND PAINS, THE RUNNING ALLOWED ME TO RELEASE MY ANXIETIES AND ANGERS IN A POSITIVE WAY.

But soon new worries cropped up. Dad had told me about the races and the satisfaction of being in shape, but he had neglected to mention that training for the quarter-mile sprint and long jump really hurt. I learned how it felt to have frequent cramps that flared up in my thighs and calves, burning like fire going through my body. Yet for all the hard work and pains, the running allowed me to release my anxieties and angers in a positive way. I could pour out all my feelings through sheer animal exertion as I rounded the last hundred yards of my quarter-mile run. Once again I was gaining control of my hyperactivity.

As I negotiated the turn on the path that wound its way through our school's back lot, I found an ease coming into my gait. I was on the downhill stretch of a three-mile run nearing the two-and-a-half-mile mark, preparing to kick in on the last half-mile to pass the ninth-grader ahead of me. For three weeks he had been running just in front of me in our workouts, and I saw no reason to allow that to continue. I began to put on the pressure as we finished the turn and headed toward the coach. As I ran past the last naked tree in the grove surrounding our course, I noticed something that pulled me up short. For a moment I forgot my opponent and slowed to get a better look. On a small branch hanging from the lowest portion of the oak was a tiny bit of green. While I passed I snapped it off for closer inspection and ran on, once more finishing just behind the now exhausted ninth-grader. I looked about and saw only the familiar bare trees surrounding our school; being a Californian and having arrived in January, I had never seen an eastern spring. The bud made me curious. Was spring on its way? I didn't have long to ponder the question because my coach was yelling at me.

"Evans, get to your group! If you think my boys have time to inspect buds during practice, you've got another thing coming. I mean to run your skinny rear off today. You got quarters [quarter-mile runs] to do, boy, until you drop!"

I called to him as I ran across the yard to my quarter group: "How soon till spring, Coach? I mean, is it really near?" I had become so accustomed to the continual gray and snow of the Maryland suburb in which we lived that I had a hard time imagining anything else.

"That's right, you California boys don't have spring, do ya?" the coach said. "Well, by my guess, give it about

two or three weeks and you won't even recognize this
place. Now, move it! To your starting positions, set—and
this one is for time, any of you jokers coming in after
seventy-seven seconds can plan on running them over,
all of them! GO!"

We were off around the first turn. While we jostled
for position, I felt a sense of excitement as I anticipated
having sun instead of snow in my face, and the sight of
all those trees in green was too much for my imagination.
It must be like a jungle around here. But my thoughts
were smothered by the rising heat of pain from my legs
as we stretched out on the back 220 heading for the final
turn. My lungs gasped for air as I struggled to keep up
with the leader, who was two years older. We finished
with groans and moans, the first five of us well ahead of
the rest of the pack. I took satisfaction in knowing that
I was almost keeping up with the ninth-graders and as
of yet had not been beaten by a classmate.

The two hours of athletic discipline we endured each
afternoon were beginning to overlap into my evenings. I
found myself hitting the books with more regularity and
motivation and with little prodding from my parents. The
season's training intensified; so too did my work habits,
and I watched my grades climb accordingly. I had
thought that the time and energy I gave to track would
detract from my studies, yet the opposite was happening.
When one area of my life received discipline, so did other
areas. I had no choice but to schedule my time because
of the commitment I had made to the track team. And,
again, a source of pride was developing.

When I received my next-to-last report card I had
straight As, a first for me and a surprise back home after
the failures earlier in the year. With the approach of
spring the attacks from my hated pair also began to di-
minish. Apparently spring fever hit them both rather
hard, and they were turning their energies in the direc-

tion of the many females on our campus. My sights were focused on the area meet, and I had little energy to devote to girls. I wanted that area championship badly, and after that maybe even the state competition.

The track ahead of me was swept clean. Its neat white lines ringed the quarter-mile length, showing us where we could and could not run. The silence of the audience only increased my anxiety. The starter had called out for us to get ready, which meant that at any moment we would be running all-out to take the area championship. The silence, after what seemed an incredibly long wait, was shattered by the report of the starting pistol and we were off. Arms and legs splayed everywhere as we made our young bodies go at their top speed; the familiar pain rose from my legs and crept into my lungs earlier than usual. I was sure someone had tossed a monkey onto my back as I rounded the final turn behind the three leaders. I had never felt so tired.

I glanced down at my feet, suspecting that someone from another school had poured sticky molasses onto my lane to slow me down, but saw only clear track whizzing by. In vain I attempted to keep the boy on my left from passing me just before we hit the finish line, but it was no use. I had come in fifth out of a field of six with no chance of qualifying for the state meet. In dejection I stumbled off the track, not even bothering to get my time from the man collecting the stats. The second heat of the quarter brought even worse results for our second runner, who almost didn't finish. The monkey that jumped on his back on the last turn was even bigger than mine.

We returned to school and made a hasty retreat to the locker room, not wishing to explain to our schoolmates that we had failed so badly in area competition. But the next day as I walked from my homeroom to my first-period class, I was met with congratulations from assorted people I had never met before. I had no idea why they were proud of me and didn't discover the reason until the end of the day, when I had time to sneak down to the front hall to our trophy case. There for all to see were the school track records that had been set the previous day. Glancing down the column, I found my name listed under the seventh grade for best 440-yard run. Although I hadn't beaten the area's best, I had managed to beat my classmates with a time of 66.9 seconds.

It certainly was nothing to boast about among track fans; the time was rather mediocre. But it was the fastest anyone in my grade had run. I took great pride in that. As I walked outside into the humid Maryland spring and unlocked my bike to ride home, I felt glad to be east. Nevertheless I was yearning to transfer to another school. I got my chance that summer as I took the entrance exam for St. Albans School for Boys.

CHAPTER 8

In the Hallowed Halls

My hands shook with anticipation as I greedily tore through the envelope bearing the St. Albans insignia on its cover and addressed from the Office of Admissions. My mother had handed me the letter as I was halfway out the door on my way to the car for a family outing, and now I was standing in the middle of our lawn excitedly extracting the letter, dying inside to know whether or not I had been accepted. During my interviews and testing I had been told that there were only four places available in the new eighth-grade class, or "second form" as it was dubbed at St. Albans, and priority went to alumni sons and the best of the applicants. I was told not to get my hopes up, but I so wanted to get into another school that I couldn't help praying and wanting with all that was in me.

From the Office of Admissions of the St. Albans School for Boys, Mt. St. Albans, Washington, D.C.

Dear James,
We are glad to inform you that we can offer you a place in the class of 1978 . . .

I couldn't believe what I had read, and I had to reread it before I allowed myself to accept the news. No more waiting for my enemies to beat me up in the halls, no more classes that I found boring because of their easy standards. I was going to St. Albans! I could hardly contain myself as I rocketed into the car, broadcasting the news to the family. There was one string attached: I must attend summer school immediately to beef up my poor English abilities. A small price to pay, I thought, for escape from the school I hated so thoroughly. My admission was the closest thing to a miracle that I had ever known: my father was not an alumnus, nor were my test grades impressive. God must have been working overtime on this one, I decided.

I was awed by the oak-paneled halls, the leaded stained-glass windows, and the arched ceilings of the old main building of my new school. My self-consciousness had waned considerably since my arrival that morning. I was not alone in my formality of coat and tie nor was my intimidated expression unusual among the other new boys entering the eighth grade. Everywhere I looked there was stone and glass, not the ugly brick of the former school with its closed-off exterior, but graced with gardens and trees. The old buildings were majestically maintained on seventy-six acres of the National Cathedral property. St. Albans had been founded in 1911 as the choirboys' school for the Cathedral, which was, and still is, being built on the highest knoll above our school. It is a massive structure, the thirteenth-largest cathedral in the world by one authority's estimate—the virgin stone still grayish white and unsoiled, glass windows where someday beautifully crafted stained glass will be placed.

I marveled at my new surroundings. The halls whispered to me of history, and I could almost feel the past generations of graduated boys passing me in the deserted yards. Many of my classmates had been going to the Cathedral's schools for most of their lives, and I found their attitudes difficult, if not impossible, to understand. They took so much of that beauty for granted, whereas I, now an eighth-grader, could hardly control myself when exploring the ancient nooks and crannies of both my school and the unfinished Cathedral. On the walls of the school hung the faded, yellowing photographs of graduating classes dating back to the school's beginning; the students' starched collars and serious poses enchanted me. *Am I actually here?* I asked myself so many times a day. Would I really never step back into my former junior high? My energy was soaring as I scoured the school, careful to leave no hall or passage unexplored.

MY ADMISSION INTO ST. ALBANS WAS THE CLOSEST THING TO A MIRACLE THAT I HAD EVER KNOWN.

The beginning of the school year brought massive quantities of work, and, with new friends to make, I found myself thoroughly engulfed in the life of St. Albans. The morning hours were dedicated to chapel, a daily routine that most students dreaded, then classes in the basics: reading, writing, and arithmetic, with the early afternoon dedicated to history and sciences. Lunch was served family style in an immaculate refectory. Our aim was to eat as much as we could and as fast as we could before the seconds ran out. Being second-formers, which meant the top level of the lower school according to the English system, we eighth-graders enjoyed certain privileges that our younger schoolmates did not. For instance,

Mrs. Martin, an indomitable woman who had spent over forty years at the institution and who was in charge of overseeing our table of twelve assorted boys, would regularly dish out the largest and first portions of food to us.

The late afternoons were for sports and study hall, both of which were required for all students. It was the aim of St. Albans to make boys fit in mind, spirit, and body; therefore sports and chapel were as inevitable as exams and textbooks. But my height and weight caught the eye of the coaching staff, who quickly took me from my lower school routine and enrolled me into the upper school football program. I was placed on the offensive line, playing with ninth- and tenth-graders, and was therefore exempt from early afternoon sports. Instead, I went immediately to study hall and then to the playing fields later in the afternoon with the older boys. I regularly received a thrashing from my opponents until I began to adjust to the subtleties and techniques behind devastating one's opponents on the line.

The table around me grew respectfully quiet. I took no notice and continued my assault upon the chicken breast in front of me, but before I could take a second bite I was in his grip. Pain shot from one shoulder blade to the other as I winced, realizing now why my companions had fallen so suddenly quiet. Two small, powerful hands bore down into my back and neck from behind, fixing me in the vice that so many of us feared and respected.

"By gosh, Evans, I see you've been lifting again!" he exclaimed. "Mrs. Martin, see to it that this boy is well fed; put some meat on this frame of his before Thursday. I hear tell this team is going to play St. Stephen's, and they'll need all the help they can get against that bunch."

The man speaking from behind me was our headmas-

ter, Canon Martin, a robust, compact Episcopal priest
who had led the school for generations and was likely to
break one's finger bones when he shook hands. An age-
less man, he stood no taller than five feet six and resembled a walking fireplug. Some thought he was about sixty
and others swore him to be eighty. His strength was legendary. No sixth-former had yet been credited with a
victory over him in arm wrestling, and he loved to demonstrate that strength through his mighty grip. He would
come up behind an unsuspecting boy and apply murderous pressure to his shoulder blades. It was considered to
be a test of sorts, and none dared wince under it. His
driving was said to be the most dangerous in Washington,
D.C., and only God's angels kept him from frequent ac-
cidents. But as a headmaster, he was unquestionably one
of the most effective men who had ever served the
school. We respected him deeply. He had a vision for
our institution and held us to strict standards, although
at times his sermons made even the most attentive lis-
tener slumber.

Leaving our table, Canon Martin sped to the podium to
offer the closing prayer before excusing us. I rubbed my
throbbing shoulders and returned to my chicken. I was
interrupted a second time by the bell that told us we
were about to be addressed. All turned attentively to the
front. Grudgingly, I left my meal to listen. "Boys," Canon
Martin began, "I've noticed recently that many of you
have been eroding our lawn and doing damage to our
flower beds. This will stop. My boys don't cut corners.
No, they do not. A St. Albans man does not cut corners
on the grass, and he doesn't cut corners in life either!
The habits you set in small things here are the habits
you will, in the future, be setting in large things else-

where. Cut the corners on the walks today, and you'll be cutting the corners in your studies tomorrow. This cutting business will stop."

With that he blessed the ended meal and excused us, which left me, still holding my piece of unfinished chicken aloft in my greasy fingers, to consider the words of the man who had just left. They had a special meaning for me.

Chuck Reinhold was in his thirties and retained much of the athletic poise of his younger days, when he had devastated the opposing ranks of defensive players who attempted to stop his drives for yardage as a running back for Pittsburgh. Chuck had the ability to make you feel worthwhile and complimented almost immediately after meeting him. The National Presbyterian Church had been without a substantial youth program for years, and it was Chuck's job as our new assistant pastor to correct that situation. He had a vision for our church, and St. Albans and its sister school, National Cathedral School, were part of it. They, along with other schools, were to be the base for a new youth group, centered at National Presbyterian Church and bringing together young people who wanted to grow in their relationship with Christ.

Chuck began organizing me and my Christian friends at St. Albans to aid him in his work. Each Wednesday morning at 6:45 we would meet at his house for Bible study, planning, and prayer. Chuck was a tireless memorizer of Scripture and saw to it that any potential leaders of his youth group did the same. It wasn't unusual to be asked in the middle of a meeting or during one of his talks to "help him out" with a verse, being asked to recite it in front of the entire group. Heaven help the kid who forgot or neglected to do his memory work that week! The embarrassing silence that followed was enough to encourage even the most reluctant member to make up for lost time and get memorizing.

Chuck, like Canon Martin, was a man totally committed to excellence in his field. For Chuck, that meant encouraging as many of us as possible to be "hot for Christ," unyielding in our discipline for God, stopping short of nothing to do what our Lord required.

The rowdy singing slowed as we quieted down to hear the message for that Sunday evening. With the finish of the song, the lean, balding man stepped in front of the gathering and waited for us to calm down. Chuck began by reading Matthew 6:33, a verse emphasizing our need to make God our first priority. Then he put the Bible down and looked at us.

"I used to have an Irish setter. Beautiful animal, he really was," he said, "but he was so high-strung that any leash, no matter how long, was too short for him. Get a twenty-yard leash and he'd be tugging twenty yards out. Just never could stay close to his master. Well, after that dog died my father gave me a beagle, which was the most obedient animal I ever had. Give him a twenty-yard leash and guess where he'd be?" There was a pause as the audience considered the possible alternatives. A seventh-grader blurted out, "If he was obedient, he'd be right next to you the whole time."

With a nod, Chuck approved her answer. "That's exactly right, Jennifer. That dog never left my side, even with a twenty-yard leash. Now I want us all to be like that beagle. There's no rule that says we can't be like the Irish setter. There are plenty of laws in the Bible that are left up to our interpretation: drinking, dating, and how to spend our time, to name a few. I've heard a lot of people saying, 'Well, the Bible doesn't say it's wrong, so it must be okay.' But that's backwards thinking. I don't want us thinking about how to skirt God's laws so we can have our fun and be free from guilt at the same time. No, I want us thinking the way my beagle thought: 'What can I do to stay as close to my master as possible?' There are lots of things in the Bible we're allowed to do, but at times many of them may be harmful to our relationship with Christ—'All things are lawful for me, but all things edify not.' So the decision is yours to make: in school and at home, are you going to be an Irish setter or a beagle for God?" And with that he sat down.

Canon Martin and Chuck Reinhold spoke the same language, a language of discipline and unflinching devotion to a goal, whether it was academic and athletic excellence or dedication to an intimate relationship with Jesus Christ. I was being bombarded in eighth and ninth grades with the kind of encouragement that built motivation. With that support, I was able to attack my learning disability on three major fronts: my social life improved markedly as I gained confidence in my ability to control my hyperactivity; academically I was pulling Bs, which was well above what I had expected; and the most obvious improvement was in my athletic ability. In running, I was finding one of my main strengths and sources of affirmation.

During the 1960 Olympics, Brooks Johnson had been, briefly, the fastest man on earth. In the first heat he won the 100-meter sprint and broke the world's record, only to be beaten in the second heat. Now this same man, our current track coach, was chasing me around the St.

> I WAS BEING BOMBARDED IN EIGHTH AND NINTH GRADES WITH THE KIND OF ENCOURAGEMENT THAT BUILT MOTIVATION.

Albans cinder track with a pair of half-inch track spikes in his hands, threatening to bury them in my rear if I did not increase my pace on the next quarter I was to run. Wisely, I picked up my speed to avoid having my track shorts perforated.

Having completed my speed workout to Brooks's satisfaction, I was ordered over to the long jump pit to begin my training. I was having trouble getting the height I needed, and Brooks said he had the remedy.

"Now, look, you fourteen-carat moron, I want you to jump driving off on your left leg while throwing up your arms to get momentum. Don't be lazy on the board, but drive through—here, like this, come here." And with that command he grabbed both my wrists and hoisted my arms as his left foot deftly smacked my right leg, sending it upward with a sting. He was giving me the general idea at the expense of my skin. "Now, Evans, do what you just did and I'll guarantee you more distance."

I jogged back to my starting point and awaited his command; with it, I sprinted down the runway and launched myself into the air. With a crash I hit the pit and jumped out, brushing the sand from my shorts. From the look on Brooks's face I could tell I had a lot of work to do. Silently he turned around and picked up a shovel from the pit box; turning back, he filled it with sand and pointed it my way. "Listen, idiot, and I'll only say it one time, you got less height that time than a pregnant duck. See this shovel, boy?" I nodded in fear and had the sick feeling that I knew what was coming. Placing the shovel over the beginning of the pit, he set it at the proper level for a well-executed jump, and began his tirade again. "I hope for your sake that you clear this shovel on your next jump, 'cause I'm not moving it if you don't. Now get your rear in gear and jump."

Obediently I jogged to my starting point, knowing full well that I had no chance of getting that high even if I had all day to try. Speeding down the runway, I tried my best and landed in the pit unscathed, realizing that at the last second he had lowered the shovel to save me from hitting it. The thought had only just passed through my mind before I was hit square in the back by a flying load of sand, the shovel's former contents. Brooks was pushing me to go all-out, even on the practice runs. With his usual laugh he turned and headed for his other train-ees, calling to me as he went to "keep working." I took his advice—I knew he'd be back.

Brooks Johnson's strength, aside from his vast experi-ence, was his care for his runners, exemplified in the amount of personal one-on-one time he spent with each of us. He regularly inspired fear, yet no one could ever accuse him of being undedicated to his athletes. Being a young ninth-grader, I was allowed to set my own sched-ule. Brooks ruled the varsity runners with an iron rod; they were potential point scorers and had to be under his steady eye. I was far from being a potential winner and was therefore being taught to enjoy track before it became a competitive struggle.

Brooks encouraged me to be an all-around type until I found my niche—he would send me one day to work with the discus throwers and the next to run long dis-tance with his two-milers. Each day after my track prac-tice I was to report to the weight room and lift. I was beginning to feel like a jack-of-all-trades, jumping from one event to the next, but without fail I ran my six miles and lifted each day. Somehow those two individual train-ing sessions gave me a pleasure that competition did not deliver. As I would lift or run on my own and at my own pace, the hyperactivity that pushed my mind haphazardly from one thought to the next and made it difficult to concentrate was eased. I could think clearly, and the once-uncontrollable buzz of energy was being used to propel me in my workouts. I was learning how to adapt my hyperactivity to my benefit: a one-time liability was becoming a resource. Working myself hard enabled me to do without Ritalin or any other medication.

After my workouts, an unfamiliar peace would settle over me, for I had expended the pent-up hyperdrive that had been accumulating over the day. Later, after my shower, I could concentrate on my studies and the continual rocking of my leg or foot that had always been part of my posture became less and less apparent. On the days that I missed a workout the old buzz would return, manifesting itself in my habitual stuttering and inability to concentrate. The more Brooks pushed me in my practices, the better I could study and the more markedly my grades rose.

> **I WAS LEARNING HOW TO ADAPT MY HYPERACTIVITY TO MY BENEFIT.**

As much as I enjoyed exercising with the track team, in competition I was a failure. I always finished my particular event dead last or thereabouts. With all the work I put in, I wondered why I didn't do better. I figured Brooks was probably wondering the same, and therefore I wasn't surprised to be summoned to his office after a particularly poor showing in the long jump during a dual meet.

I knew what he was going to say. He was going to call me a fourteen-karat mess-up and bawl me out for choking at the meets. The anxiety had been building all afternoon, ever since my buddy Doug had informed me in an ominous voice that Brooks wanted to see me. Doug was curious to know whether I wanted to have our chaplain, Father Downes, serve me last rites. I declined the offer and walked to my coach's office wondering how I might escape the inevitable.

I found Brooks lounging in a chair, explaining the art of starting to one of his promising sprinters. I waited my turn, wishing I had taken up lacrosse instead of track. Before I could sneak away, I found myself facing the man sitting in a chair opposite his desk. Brooks closed the door and resumed his seat. He never closes the door, even when he bawls out one of us. *Oh, help, I must really be in for it!* I thought.

With what little breath I could muster I babbled, "You wanted to t-to t-t-to see me, Coach?"

"Yea, Evans, I wanted to tell you how impressed I am with you."

I tried to comprehend what I had heard. He had said the exact opposite of what I was expecting. Was he being sarcastic, setting me up for the kill?

"Kid, I realize you haven't been all that successful in winning points for the team. You might be a little down about that, but you're the most disciplined man on our team and a real asset. Now, I've got some boys out there who by the gift of God can run mighty fast, and I intend to see to it that they demolish our opponents. But, mind you, that's natural talent I'm talking about. They were born fast. You—well, Evans, no one could ever accuse you of being born fast, but what you've got is made, not born: discipline. Keep it, and don't feel outclassed by those runners even when they do wipe you off the track. I've watched you this year. What I saw lacking in ability was made up in discipline. You haven't missed a workout yet and when you run you put all you've got into it. I never have to push you to do your distance. I think you actually enjoy those weight and distance workouts, don't you?"

I nodded, not quite sure I was the boy he was describing.

"You probably won't win many races for us," he went on, this time drawing a toothpick from his pocket, speaking and chewing on it simultaneously. "But you should be proud of yourself. You're becoming a strong, disciplined kid—nothing to be ashamed of in any of that." With that he dismissed me with a wave of his hand.

I walked back to the library, trying to absorb what I had just been told. A tingling sensation shot through me from my feet to my head. I could hardly contain the satisfaction I felt. If I couldn't compete with the rest of them on ability, I'd do it with discipline. That was my strength, dyslexia and hyperkinesia had taught me that, and I began to feel grateful that I was an LD kid. It seemed to me that I was beginning to reap benefits from a disorder that most people considered a handicap.

CHAPTER 9

Teachers Who Teach the Hard Way

"You are to read, learn, and inwardly digest the material that I am passing out to you. Do you understand, little boys?"

The man standing before us was an institution in his own right. Ferdinand B. Ruge had been St. Albans's top English teacher for over forty years and had instructed two generations of pupils in the *art* of writing. Now he was turning his attention to his latest tenth-grade class, and his legendary course (we were promised by those who had survived it) would be our most difficult and demanding yet.

"I need someone dumb, but conscientious, to help me pass out these papers. You, what's your name? Yes, of course, Evans. Here, pass these out, boy." I took the heavy sheaf of mimeographed papers from the seventy-five-year-old in the three-piece suit and began passing them out to my less-than-enthusiastic classmates. We had heard too many horror stories to be relaxed on this first day of Mr. Ruge's class. As he began to call the roll, he read our names slowly and took a good look at us.

His wire-rimmed spectacles gleamed menacingly from their perch on his big nose.

"Hand, Colton Hand. Yes, there you are. Now, who's Hardison, where's this unfortunate lad, Hardison? Ah, yes. Mr. Hardison, I did not say that you could take off your jacket, did I? And do straighten your tie, boy, I fail boys with unstraightened ties. Now, that's better. Oh, no! Not another Goodrich! It must be a lie. Didn't I teach both your brothers, Goodrich, and your father and uncle? Am I to be plagued again by yet another? You'd think four were enough. No doubt you're as dumb as the rest— now what's your name? Is it Craig or George?"

"I'm Tom, sir," the tall boy to my right mumbled, waiting for the assault to begin again.

"What's that, boy? You must speak up! Old men can't hear as you young folk can. Now what's it, boy, did you say George?"

"No, sir, it's Tom. George is my father."

"Well, George or Craig or whatever your name is, I'm going to give a little test to you all and I want you to give yourself five extra points on it, because you're going to need all the help you can get, as a Goodrich." With that our commander passed out a single-page test.

A boy in the back of the room raised his hand. "Sir, Mr. Ruge, sir."

"Yes, what is it, boy?"

"Sir, I don't think it's fair for Tom to be getting five extra points on the test," the brave kid from the back piped up.

"Fair? Who said anything about fair, boy? Life isn't fair, and I have no intention of being fair, either." And with that, Mr. Ruge proceeded to give us our first test.

"Now, boys, just read the instructions and finish as quickly as you can," he demanded.

We dove into the test, knowing full well that Mr. Ruge was considered the hardest grader in the school. As I scanned the instructions, I figured that the test was self-explanatory and so plunged into what I considered to be a nearly impossible English questionnaire. Midway through it, I happened to glance up and noticed that four of my classmates were sitting by calmly, looking at the rest of us with sly grins on their faces. At his desk, Mr. Ruge looked as if some wonderful joke were in the making and could hardly wait to spring it on his unsuspecting students. Glancing back at my test after I saw the boy next to me feverishly completing the last question, I began again, ignoring the four who seemed to be in on Ruge's surprise.

He could contain himself no longer. Jumping up from his seat, Mr. Ruge cried: "My gracious, the city should pay me 15 percent more for teaching you! They do that, you know, they pay all teachers who instruct the mentally retarded 15 percent more. Who actually finished the test? Raise your hands." Having barely finished the last question by guesswork, I, with the vast majority of my class, raised my hand quickly. He glared at us. "How dare you 'fess up to such an ignominious accomplishment? Bellinger, read the directions to these poor boys."

John B. Bellinger, III, one of the four who had finished long before I was even close to doing the first question, coolly read over the directions to the class. The last paragraph of the directions stated: "This test is designed to gauge your ability to read directions. Put down your pencils, fold your hands and do not answer any of the questions below." Like the rest of my class, I hadn't bothered to read the instructions thoroughly. In my haste to get started, I had scanned only the first few paragraphs, assuming the test was self-explanatory.

"Now, little boys, do you feel just a bit stupid? Well, if you don't, you should!" Turning to one of my classmates who had answered the test questions at considerable length, Mr. Ruge stated dryly, "Stuart, you must be the dumbest boy I've ever seen. Took the bait, hook, line, and sinker, didn't you?" Stuart sat totally speechless in his shame.

As we filed out of class that first day, I felt as if I had been battered in a war. The amount of English homework Mr. Ruge assigned was staggering. Along with the written work, we were instructed to begin memorizing "Ruge Rules," the mimeographed sheets containing the paraphrased sacred laws by which we were to write from then on. I looked down at my already-filled notebook. "How am I going to memorize these rules before I even understand what they all mean?" I groaned to my friend Tom, the Goodrich who had been chosen for abuse.

> AS WE FILED
> OUT OF
> CLASS THAT
> FIRST DAY, I
> FELT AS IF I
> HAD BEEN
> BATTERED IN
> A WAR.

"Thomas, have you seen the rules we have to learn for tomorrow? Is this guy for real? Check this one out: 'Some, let, bit, get, thing: these words you shall not use; they are meaningless and undescriptive.'"

Tom nodded grimly. "My dad had this guy and it only gets worse," he remarked. "If we fail him, we don't graduate. Do you think he's ever going to learn my name?"

If the massive amount of work plus the abuse we received in class wasn't enough, there was still more to come. We were informed the next day that each of us was to make an appointment to see Mr. Ruge in his office. He wanted to discuss our individual English weaknesses with us. A silent groan shot through us all at that announcement. It was bad enough to be picked on in a full class, without having him rail at us one-on-one. I made my appointment early, wanting to get the inevitable over as quickly as possible.

The two-page paper lay before him. My first Ruge assignment was marked with his red pen on each page, with exact quotations from our English manual, citing page number and reference that I was to read to correct my numerous mistakes. I sat before him, breaking out in a sweat, awaiting the ax.

"Evans, this paper is a mess," he began. "Why, I see misspellings and errors that a fourth-grader would be embarrassed to make. What's wrong, boy, got some disease?" he probed in jest.

Hesitantly I began. "Well, sir, I do have a learning disability . . . They call it dyslexia . . . and it does make it tough for me to write at times, but I—"

Mr. Ruge waved off my excuse and removed his spectacles. "How long have you known about this dyslexia, and what work have you done to date to correct it?" he asked in a milder tone.

I related my story to him as he sat patiently listening with closed eyes. When I had finished, he instructed me to correct my mistakes carefully and be sure to hand in my corrected paper to him the next day. I was dismissed from his office.

Had I actually seen a gentle side of Mr. Ruge? Why had he listened so quietly, not interrupting with his usual gibes? As I turned in my corrected paper the next day, I noticed my name scrawled on his appointment board. The handwriting was his. Mr. Ruge taught only two classes a day; the rest of his time he spent one-on-one, hammering English into his tenth-graders. He was not paid for his extra time with us, but volunteered it. Each day three or four boys would receive the counseling session of their lives from a man who prided himself on taking a fine-tooth comb to their work; no misspelled word went unnoticed, no dangling modifier was left un-changed. I found myself being summoned in almost weekly, many more times than any of my classmates. As he and I attacked my weaknesses day after day, my hand often became sore from rewriting words I had misspelled dozens of times.

"You may be a dyslexic, little boy," he chided me one afternoon, "but no one can claim ignorance when there's a dictionary nearby. Now use it and write 'Renaissance' fifty times and atone for your sins."

I was beginning to see the real Mr. Ruge, the teacher so many said was the best they'd had. Before our coun-seling sessions had begun, I had thought they were talk-ing about another person; but now I, too, was beginning to see the soft side of him. I sensed that his gruff exterior was a mask for a very sensitive and generous heart. He was from the old school, sure enough, where teachers were dictatorial rulers of their students; yet he cared, and he proved that care in the free gift of his time to us. Nevertheless, his gibes could hurt.

I WONDERED IF I WOULD EVER FIND ANYTHING EASY.

"Now, little boys, there's a job out there somewhere for Evans; do you know what that job is?" he fired at the entire class one day. "Ditch dig-ging, Evans! That's right, it's a good, honest job. No boy can graduate from this school without passing my course, and your average is 56.4. You're failing, boy, though if I were you, I'd be thankful that I wasn't Mr. Donald there, smirking at your poor fortune from across the room. Mr. Donald's average is 46.3, so he's failing even worse than you are." The boy singled out by Mr. Ruge lost his smile immediately and replaced it with a look of imminent doom. Mr. Ruge hadn't given back any of our tests yet, so all of us were in the dark about our standing. At last the truth was surfacing, and even with my extra sessions I was doing some of the worst work in my class.

"Donald, Evans, we have names for boys like you: losers!" he raged. In my mind I was myself being drummed out of the beloved school and sent back to the public school system, branded an academic reject. I was about as low as I could be that day, and the fact that another boy was a few points lower than I didn't give much comfort. How many grades are lower than an F-minus?

Fighting back with what little I had, I began attending Mr. Ruge's Saturday sessions, which were designed to complement his weekday teaching. I also signed up for his summer reading course, which added a few precious points to my grade. But that whole semester I was in limbo between passing and failing, with the fear of being tossed back into my old junior high continually haunting my mind. That fear drove me all the harder in my studies. Remembering what Brooks Johnson had said about my discipline, I put that strength to work for me in Ruge's class. It was the only reliable tool I had.

Coming from one of Mr. Ruge's murderous sessions, I passed the lower-level bulletin board where the theater tryout schedules were posted. One of my older football buddies, Hank Sommers, a huge tackle from Ohio, had mentioned that he was trying out that day. I was curious to see him act; it was said that he was as good on the stage as on the football field. As I quietly opened the theater door, I saw a group of boys and girls, maybe one hundred in all, jamming the front of the theater, waiting their turn to audition. I found Hank and sat next to him, inquiring when he was up. "I'm on call in about ten minutes," he said. "What are you doing here, Jimmy? I thought you'd still be slaving away with old Ruge."

"No more Ruge for today. I came down to try out too," I surprised myself by saying. Why had I said it? Three minutes before I had no intention of trying out for a show. Before I could reconsider my words, I was dragged up in front of Mrs. Witt and Ted Walch, the theater directors, to read a part from *The Crucible,* Arthur Miller's drama inspired by the witch-hunts of the McCarthy era in American political history. St. Albans believed in presenting shows of substance and this one was no exception.

The script shook in my hand as I fumbled and stuttered through my lines. I marveled at the effortless way Hank read his assigned part, lowering his voice into a rich bass of added expression. I felt totally outclassed, embarrassed by the nagging stutter that turned sentences into a jumble of vowels and consonants tripping over each other. I left the stage feeling worse than I had before coming into the theater. Quietly, I slipped out and headed to my sports locker to suit up for football practice. I longed to take my day's aggressions out on the players I'd be facing on the line. Crashing into an opponent was an incredible release at such times. Walking toward the football field, I chewed on my mouth guard as I wondered if I would ever find anything easy.

"Hit that sled, now, move it. Hit and roll, hit and roll, that's rights. Give it 100 percent—and don't you ever walk back to the line! Run!"

Our line coach drove us hard that day, and I loved getting back at my frustration and anger as I let loose on the stuffed dummy in front of me, driving with all my force into it, making it double over from the impact. A large, powerful hand slapped me from behind; it was

Hank Sommer's familiar greeting. "Jimmy, the actor," he said. "Yes, my fellow grunge brothers, you are looking at an actor to be, stutters and all." The linemen around us nudged each other.

"What are you talking about, Hank?" I replied. "I totally messed up on that stage today."

A large friend of Hank's who had also attended the tryout broke line as our coach gave us a breather from the hitting. "Now, Evans, no one will deny that you are the deserved stutter king," he said, "but Walch and Witt want to hear you again. You made the callbacks, idiot!" The lineman headed for the hoses as I was left standing by the dummies, wondering if it was all a joke. Had I actually been called back? Surely my stuttering was a barrier to acting!? Before I could pursue the thought, the whistles of our coaches summoned us back to teamwork. We were doing quick calls on the defensive alignment, and they demanded all our concentration, but I was going to question Hank in the locker room about the acting deal later.

Quick calls entailed shifting position to the left or right as instructed by our "monster man," a roving defensive back who commanded the rest of the defensive players. It was his responsibility to position us by reading the offensive team's intent through their formation. If he were to call, "Stack check, monster right," then it was my responsibility as a left tackle to move left. We began our drills with new alignments assigned for the week; not only were the quick calls complicated but they constantly shifted.

The call came—"Stack check blitz, monster right"— and with it much movement, as players jumped to their spots on the line. I found myself crouched, head up, opposite the offensive center, ready to blast off and plug any runner who tried to come through my area. My hands were suddenly kicked out in front on me, throwing me facedown into the dust of the field. Something told me I had moved to the wrong position, and one look at my coach, who had kicked my hands out from under me, confirmed that fear. "Evans, don't you ever move the right way? If it's 'stack check blitz, with the monster to your right,' then where do you set yourself?" he demanded.

Thinking for a moment, I answered, "I should go to my left, sir." A nervous silence came over the rest of my teammates and I knew I was in trouble.

"Then why didn't you move to your left?"

Embarrassed, I realized that I had jumped to my right and ended up fully two positions away from my assigned position. "I don't know, Coach. I guess I got confused," I replied.

"Dyslexia again, huh, Evans? Well, try to think it out better next time," he said in a milder tone.

Even in football my disability followed me. I often found it very difficult to coordinate motor activity, especially under pressure; and left/right commands were deadly. I was continually jumping the wrong way when commanded. The following year, when I played on the first-string team, my coach had a defensive back behind me tap me in the direction I was supposed to move whenever I was set incorrectly. Unfortunately it had taken about a year of repeated mistakes and corrections to force me to tell the coaching staff about my learning disability. Once they were aware of my problem, we made up for it with compensation drills: a piece of tape on my shoe to tell me which way was left, a helpful defensive back keeping an eye out for me, and, at times, extra practice sessions for the whole team—"Just so Evans can get it straight."

As we filed back into the locker room after a hard-hitting practice, I made my way to the front where Hank's locker was located. "Are you pulling my leg on this callback list?" I asked him as he was struggling simultaneously with a tight pair of shoulder pads and a bent cleat.

"Jimmy, would I kid you? They really want to see you tomorrow for another reading. And this time, don't get so uptight. Most of your dumb stuttering happens because you take things too seriously. Ease up tomorrow, and do me a favor. Take a shower, real quick. I think something died on your jersey—it's turning green!"

"Very funny, Pretzel Head. Look, you've got to give me a hand on this thing tomorrow," I implored.

"I'll do what I can, Jimmy, okay?" He returned to struggling with his cleat.

I walked back to my locker, excited by the prospect of acting. In the shower, while washing off the sweat and mud caked on my calves, I tried to imagine what it would be like

> IT HAD TAKEN ABOUT A YEAR OF REPEATED MISTAKES AND CORRECTIONS TO FORCE ME TO TELL THE COACHING STAFF ABOUT MY LEARNING DISABILITY.

to act in front of the crowds that usually attended our school performances. Among private schools, St. Albans had one of the best acting departments in the country. It had merged with the drama department of the National Cathedral School, which gave us a large staff of directors and assistants for such a small school. We had the benefit of working closely with some of the finest semiprofessional theater people in the area. During the summer Ted Walch directed a Shakespeare company that brought a group of professional actors together with a few amateurs from our school. Understandably, I was excited about the possibility of being involved, even in the smallest way, with such serious-minded actors and directors.

I arrived a few minutes late for the callbacks that crisp October afternoon. A tinge of yellow was beginning to appear on the leaves of the giant oaks surrounding our schoolgrounds. Being a Californian at heart, I still marveled at eastern winters; the seasonal changes were always exciting to me, and fall was the best. During football practice woodsmoke from nearby homes curled into the air, and the evening chill felt good against hot muscles— especially after the sweltering D.C. summers.

In the theater I sat next to Hank again, wondering about the format of the callbacks. Would I have to read alone in front of all these people? Decidedly, the group was smaller than yesterday's masses, but I noticed five girls from NCS sitting in the front row. As a tenth-grader I was still unaccustomed to seeing girls on our campus because coed courses didn't begin in earnest until the eleventh grade, when many of the National Cathedral and St. Albans classes merged. The proximity of the girls made me all the more anxious.

A list of names was called out and several of us were herded onstage. We were to read the lead roles, so both directors wanted to be sure we looked good together. Satisfied with the appearance of their choices, the directors called us up again and again to read various parts. I began to enjoy the role I was most often chosen to read: Judge Hawthorne was one of the play's evil prosecutors. It wasn't surprising to find Hank being called to read the lead role of Judge Danforth, his huge frame easily taking on the authoritarian judge's manner.

I liked this friend of mine very much. In a way I saw Hank as the big brother I had missed in La Jolla and now in D.C. On the football field he would often take me aside and offer helpful hints on the various techniques of devastating an opponent. In the weight room we were lifting buddies, pushing one another to maximum lifts. Even in the spring we were often together. We both were interested in track and especially the shotput and discus throwing; as usual, Hank could easily outthrow me in any of my events. Now we were auditioning together, and I was grateful for his presence. Here was an upper-classman who did the things I did, did them much better, in fact, and seemed to enjoy helping me succeed. At times I found myself wishing Hank could be a real brother. Dan and Tim were in California most of the time, and I was lonesome for that kind of camaraderie. For the present, however, it was enough to have him helping me out on callbacks.

The script dangled loosely from his hand as he finished his last line. Confidence almost oozed from his pores. Hank glanced over at me and smiled, noticing my white knuckles as I gripped my script. "Jimmy, relax," he whispered as an actress across the stage made her entrance. "You're going to tear the script if you hold it any tighter. And loosen up your posture; you look like you've got a steel rod up your back!"

I gave him a mournful glance, but before I could respond it was time for my line. I was so surprised by the suddenness of it that I really didn't have time to get nervous or prepare to read. To my amazement the words flowed forth without a single stutter. As the reading went on, I discovered that the less I thought about acting, the easier and smoother it was. By the end of the auditions I regretted leaving the stage, so thoroughly had I enjoyed the reading.

"The cast list will be posted tomorrow morning by eleven A.M.," Mr. Walch announced, "and those of you who don't make it are encouraged to work on the technical part of the show. We need much work there. Those who are picked will be at rehearsal tomorrow night by seven P.M. sharp." Ted Walch was a short, lean man with a balding head and quick eyes. His expressive hands were always in motion as he skillfully guided his actors from one point on the stage to the next. There was something of the cavalier about him, and that made him one of the most popular teachers in both schools. His associate, Mrs. Witt, who was primarily responsible for the Miller performances, was a mother figure for her actors. It wasn't uncommon to find her directing a rehearsal and knitting at the same time, giving creative instructions between stitches. But she was no pushover. Let an actor be late or drop a line that he should have mastered long ago, and he would quickly discover the mettle of the woman who sat demurely before him.

The next day we gathered in front of the cast list, finding our names and the corresponding roles. Those who did not make it left disappointedly to sign up for technical positions. I came running down the stairs toward the cast list in time to see Hank leaning against the wall grinning at me. He greeted me with, "Well, Judge Hawthorne, seems as if you're now an actor. Witt picked half the offensive line to be in this show."

"Judge Danforth, I presume?" I responded and he nodded. We scanned the cast list looking for familiar names. Hank was right about the football team—about six members of the varsity squad were in the play. Many of them, in fact, were first-rate Shakespearean actors.

My schedule was crammed with activity. With Mr. Ruge's course and my four others, plus football, play rehearsal in the evenings, Saturdays with Mr. Ruge in his special catch-up class, and my church duties, there was precious little time for home. It wasn't unusual for me to be at school from 7:30 A.M. to 11:00 P.M. daily. Church and Mr. Ruge took up the weekend days, while my weekend evenings were reserved for dates and parties. As I look back now, I can scarcely believe the schedule I maintained during those years. But my first show, *The Crucible*, only whetted my appetite for more acting, and soon I was auditioning for the winter show.

This time I was the first to make it to the newly posted cast list for our winter show, *A Streetcar Named Desire*, by Tennessee Williams. Glancing down the list, I was dumbfounded. Again I searched it thoroughly. There was no mistake. I was not on it. Now it was my turn to sign up for the tech crew. Was my acting career to be cut short? Depressed, I wondered if my stuttering and slurred speech had caused my downfall. I walked down the stairs to the theater office below the stage to inquire about possibilities for tech work.

The director's assistant, Ann Crow, met me. "Jamie, sorry about your not getting into the play," she said. "Mr. Walch would like to speak to you tomorrow. Can you make it about 1:15 down here?"

I told her that I was to have my last meeting with Mr. Ruge at that time.

"Why don't you come down after that session and you can see Ted then," she said. Then she added: "Jamie, are you having troubles with Mr. Ruge's class? If you are, you're certainly not alone." Ann was the kind of woman you could talk to, and we sat there for about twenty minutes bemoaning the rigors of English under Ruge and sipping strong tea that was always brewing in the theater office. I liked being there. The office gave me a feeling of belonging and being special. There was a magical aura about everything in the theater.

The door slammed behind us as Ted Walch darted into the office, his scarf billowing behind him as he tossed his Gatsby cap onto the hat rack in the corner. Gathering up a volume of Shakespeare and some manuals, he began to climb the stairs, late as usual for his class. On the way, he poured himself a cup of steaming tea and gulped it greedily. Speaking to Ann but intending his comment to be heard by both of us, he said, "Little does the lad next to you realize it, but a miracle is about to unfold. We at Trapier Theater are about to make a sow's ear into a silk purse." Pointing in my direction, he went on, "You, my boy, are the sow's ear, soon to be our silk purse." And with that he scampered up the stairs to his waiting class.

> I DISCOVERED THAT THE LESS I THOUGHT ABOUT ACTING, THE EASIER AND SMOOTHER IT WAS.

Ann answered my questioning look with a wry smile. "You are in for a rare treat," she said. She would say no more. I would have to wait till after my appointment with Mr. Ruge to have my curiosity satisfied.

The small office of Ferdinand B. Ruge, littered with papers, was by then familiar to me. I was only slightly nervous, which was far more relaxed than on that first day when the old man before me had seemed such a terror. I now considered him a friend who, despite his chiding and gibes, had our best interests firmly in mind. After a pause he closed the gradebook he had been studying since my arrival and fixed his gaze on me.

"Evans, all English teachers should be shot. Do you know why? We are murderers. We keep the language from evolving. We hold it stagnant. We set rules to write by and let none stray beyond those bounds. We kill all creativity in young bloods like you who would make our language adapt to this changing world. Yes, boy, we all should be taken out and shot immediately. But since there are great books written in the present-day English, I see it as my job to keep alive and pure the language in which they are written."

With a rasping cough that shook his sturdy frame, he resumed: "Now you in your time with me have done all you can to pervert that language. You have misspelled words that I thought were impossible to misspell. *Does*, boy, is spelled with an *e* in the middle, not at the end. The other way is *dose*, i.e., a portion. You have placed more dangling participles in a sentence than I have seen any boy before you place, and your wordy, wooden style is enough to turn my father in his grave. As my Jewish friends would say, you have *chutzpah*, which means unmitigated gall in the English."

Despite his usual monologue I knew he was not angry. In his own way he was leading up to good news. Was it possible that he wasn't going to fail me?

"Despite all your egregious sins against my profession, I have, out of the goodness of my heart, decided to pass you with a C-plus for the term." An audible sigh escaped from my lungs and I felt pounds lift from my shoulders. The ghosts of my former junior high slipped forever out the window. I would not have to return there—or go to any other public school, for that matter.

"I've been watching you, young man," he went on, "and I must tell you something. In my forty years of teaching I have seen my share of brilliant and disciplined students. Now I would not call you brilliant, no, that I would not, but hardworking you are. Don't let this go to your head, but you have been the most dedicated, hardworking student I have ever had. You will probably never be a good English student. Your grade is representative of your effort more than your actual academic performance, but hardworking you are, and if I were you . . ."

His voice droned on in that small office. I sat there, not sure how to take such a compliment, especially from a man who was not known for giving them. Half an hour ago I had bombed out of a show, and now I was getting the compliment of a lifetime. I was on an emotional rollercoaster, uncertain whether to cry or laugh. I headed down the stairs toward Ted Walch's underground office trying to make sense out of it all.

CHAPTER 10

Acting Takes Center Stage

The houselights flickered and then dimmed, the signal for the audience in the 300-seat auditorium to take their places for the opening of the show. I stood backstage watching anxiously as quiet settled over the group out front. A muffled giggle came from the thickening shadows behind me; an angry glance from my companion silenced the squeaks. Chris McIsaac and I, now both seniors, returned our eyes to the darkness ahead of us.

Silently the actors in the first scene of *The Prime of Miss Jean Brodie* crept onstage, unnoticed by the audience. In a moment the play would start. Quietly we let drop the inner curtain from which we had been spying and sat together against the wall. I shooed the underclassmen away with a wave of my hand; their incessant chatter was getting on my nerves. Besides, they weren't on until the second act and had no business here.

I pictured the scene in front of the curtain where, swathed in stage light, a nun was recounting her early life as Jean Brodie's pupil to a reporter. I had two scenes to go until I entered, Chris just one, and waiting together helped to still the preplay shakes. With a grin Chris asked if I planned to try out for the winter show. It was a question neither of us had to answer verbally. We both knew we were in the running for the lead in Shakespeare's *Pericles*, soon to be directed by our seasoned instructor, Ted Walch. I liked Chris and hated to be in such heated competition with him over a role. He was admittedly the better actor, but I had height on my side, which helped in romantic leads.

The darkness deepened as the first scene ended and the tech crew scampered to change sets, their black uniforms making them almost invisible in the gloom. I marveled at the noiselessly passing figures burdened with furniture from onstage. How they did it so quietly was beyond me. I remarked that the knickers were just Chris's style, and he shot me a trembling grin as he paused at the curtain, waiting for the lights to mark his entrance. In a more serious tone I whispered: "Break a leg, Lowther! Heck, it's only a full house." With that he was gone, striding onto the stage with his Scottish cap twirling in his hand and singing a jig, which marked him as the play's choirmaster. He played Lowther expertly. How in the world am I going to beat him out for the part of Pericles? I worried.

As the curtains offstage closed after Chris's entrance, the darkness settled on me again. It was a long scene, and I was in no rush to stretch out. Sitting hunched against the cinder-block wall, I thought back to the first shows I had done there. Counting carefully, I figured them to be ten in all, not including the coming Shakespearean production. Had I really been in ten shows? A great deal had been accomplished since tenth grade. I felt at home sitting in my usual pre-entrance corner; it afforded me the peace that the changing rooms below did not have, and I could wait for my entrances in relative seclusion, free of distractions.

Unwinding, I let my memory take me back to all that had transpired with Ted Walch. It had changed so much of my life.

"Mr. Walch, what did you mean by calling me a 'sow's ear'? Was that a cut or something?" I had probed cautiously.

The director took his time answering. Finally he said, "Jamie, you were almost picked for the lead in *The Crucible*. Did you know that?"

Amazed, I shook my head. "I didn't think you had heard," he said. "You've got good presence onstage, but the staff and I reconsidered when we took into account your lack of experience and your speech impediment." That was the first time I had heard my stuttering called a "speech impediment." It sounded serious. "What I meant by calling you a sow's ear," he resumed, "was that most directors wouldn't consider you for a part at all, let alone a lead. You simply speak too fast and stutter too much. There are many types of speech impediments, and I don't think yours is terribly serious, although I can tell you're rather embarrassed by it."

Nodding, I agreed that it was a source of a great deal of frustration. "Mr. Walch, it always hits me when I least want it to, especially when I'm nervous. At parties it's a killer. Have you ever tried to ask a girl to dance, tripping over *d*s and *w*s? *W*s are my downfall, sir," I added.

"Yes, I've noticed you have more trouble speaking when pressure hits. That's a good sign, though. The people I have the most trouble with are the ones who stutter even when they're relaxed. You, I think, I can help. Want to become a silk purse?"

"A silk purse, sir?" I could see it now—my football coach already had strange ideas about his linemen acting.

He was going to have a hard time when I told him I was going to become a silk purse. "Well, sir, maybe if I could think about it and get back to you . . ."

"Look, Jamie, it's just a figure of speech we use around here. What I'm suggesting is that we train you to overcome your speech impediment, teach you how to speak c-l-e-a-r-l-y and d-i-s-t-i-n-c-t-l-y," he replied, stretching the words out as far as they could go. "That way, you get a good voice and we get a new actor. Mrs. Witt will work with you during this show and I'll take over in the winter and spring."

> **WHAT I DIDN'T CONSIDER WAS THE TREMENDOUS AMOUNT OF TIME I WOULD HAVE TO DEVOTE TO MY VOICE.**

His suggestion made me ache for the day when I would be able to speak like Hank, using my voice as a tool instead of being embarrassed by it. I was tired of being ribbed about my stammer, and I was willing to become a "silk purse" if it would get rid of my impediment. What I didn't consider was the tremendous amount of time I would have to devote to my voice. Mr. Walch meant business and was willing to sink hours of his time each week into private voice sessions with me, settling for nothing less than 100 percent of my effort in return.

Stretching out on the black-painted floor of the stage, I loosened my tie and awaited my instructions. Ted Walch sat below in the second row preparing to take me through our usual voice exercises before our diction work began. I had been working with him for a year, ever since my first appearance in *The Crucible* back in the tenth grade. Relaxing my tense muscles after a long day in the classroom usually took me a good fifteen minutes. Until I had thoroughly loosened up, there was no sense attempting any voice work; my stuttering would immediately surface if I allowed my body to tighten up, constricting my vocal cords. Our first exercise was designed to develop my diaphragm muscles to give me breath control while also teaching me to meter my speaking rate.

"Now, take a deep breath, hold it and exhale. Again . . . a deep breath and—wrong! Jimmy, the purpose of this is to develop what muscle?" Ted Walch impatiently queried from his seat, "How long have we been at this?"

"A year, sir, and it's designed to train my diaphragm," I answered, knowing well what I had done wrong, but certain I was going to hear it carefully explained to me again.

The lecture began: "Jimmy, when I instructed you to inhale, I saw your chest rise—your *chest*, boy! Actors don't breathe from their chests . . . they breathe from their diaphragms so they can project with unrestricted force, never running out of breath, never rushing their WORDS!" On "words" he squeezed his diaphragm and almost blasted the clock off the far wall with his volume. I got the idea. "Try it again, and this time concentrate. Inhale, slowly, let me see that diaphragm rise, yes, yes, now hold it. Good! Exhale, now again, inhale and begin please."

Filling my lungs full of air until the pressure squeezed my gut, I prepared to begin counting. Our goal was to reach one hundred on one breath, with each number clearly enunciated and evenly projected, with no rushing toward the end. It was nearly impossible, or so I had found it to be at the beginning of the year. Now I was having some success with it. I was determined to reach one hundred by the end of our warmup session. "Ninety-six . . . ninety-seven . . . ninety-eight . . ." With that, I could say no more and gasped for air, my red face returning to its normal winter pallor. The ceiling spun above me as my fingers began to tingle from lack of oxygen. It was the closest I had come to reaching one hundred without rushing or slurring! I sat up slowly and found Mr. Walch grinning at my near accomplishment.

Next it was time for tongue twisters. "Repeat after me: 'The lawyer's awfully awkward daughter ought to be taught to draw.'" I did as I was told and then repeated it. By my eighth try I had satisfied him, and we went on to my next twister: "The quick red fox jumped over the lazy brown dog." After some fifteen minutes of reciting tongue twisters and diction exercises, I was warmed up enough to begin my real assignment, reciting selections from Shakespeare.

"James, William Shakespeare was the greatest playwright of our language and millennium. Be forewarned, boy, I do not tolerate his words being stuttered and stammered over. No such abuse will be allowed in my theater. You may begin. What is the assignment for today?"

I had been asked to memorize the twenty-eight lines of Jacques's speech from *As You Like It*, chronicling the seven ages of man. Hesitantly I prepared myself, only to be cut short by Walch before I even opened my mouth. "Evans, look at yourself, it's all wrong!" he fired at me. "You look as if you're getting ready to take on the Landon offensive line. Loosen up. Remember, your problem is allowing yourself to become too tense, and that drives your stuttering through the ceiling. Relax your body and your voice will automatically follow. Paint me a scene before you give your speech. All right, where is Jacques now, just moments before delivering his line?"

Closing my eyes I transported myself to the forest where, four hundred years ago, Jacques, the melancholy philosopher, sitting by a fire in a dark clearing, gave his speech. I painted the entire scene for Walch. Then I moved from describing the scene to reciting the lines.

"All the world's a stage, and all the men and women merely players: They have their exits and their entrances; and one man in his time plays many parts, his acts being seven ages." I recited my first twelve lines until Walch stopped me and asked: "Jamie, where are you now? Have you moved, or are you still seated by the fire?"

Thinking a moment, I replied: "Yeah, I've moved, I'm circling the fire now. . . ." I began to point to people I "saw," describing the scene further.

"Now, with that in mind, finish the speech," Walch directed. Again and again we went through the monologue, building the character and setting the scene more and more realistically. Engrossed in my acting, I had lost track of the time and was startled when the class bell rang. My imaginary world evaporated instantly, and with it went Jacques and his melancholy mood. Ted Walch stood up. Picking up my jacket and books while I straightened my tie, I awaited his final criticisms. I felt it had been a good session and wanted my inclination confirmed.

"Jamie, you didn't stutter or slur once, not once, when you had set the scene and were concentrating on the character. If I can only get you to forget yourself and relax, we'll have your stuttering problem licked. When you forgot that I was listening, you forgot to stutter as well. For some reason your stuttering is linked to your audience. Get your mind off the audience, devalue them, it's the character that's important, not them. Try it in real life, too. If you aren't worried about making a good impression on people, you won't feel so pressured, and stuttering will become a thing of the past."

As I left the theater, I wondered why I always stuttered more when I was under pressure and whether I really did

overvalue my audience. Later, I would find that Ted
Walch had been right.

Dr. Lee Travis has been a good friend to three generations
of Evanses. The eighty-year-old psychiatrist and speech
pathologist began Fuller Seminary's counseling program,
which is one of the best-regarded seminary psychology
departments in the country. Sitting with him in his office,
I could see palm trees swaying in the smoggy distance.
On the advice of my mother back in Washington, D.C.,
I had made an appointment to speak with Dr. Travis on
our next excursion to L.A. The serious illness of my
grandfather had brought me back to the West Coast long
before I had anticipated, yet I was somehow squeezed
into the doctor's busy schedule for a two-hour consult-
ation. I came wanting to get to the bottom of my stuttering, and although I had received three years of
intensive voice work with the St. Albans drama department, I was still having difficulty. I was curious to learn
about the physiological causes behind my stuttering. Did
dyslexia and hyperkinesia put an impossible barrier between me and clear speech?

I learned more about myself during that two-hour conversation than from all the research I had been able to
do on my own. "Jamie, your particular problem in speech
is possibly centered in the left lobe of your brain," Dr.
Travis began. I repressed an immediate desire to feel my
head for any abnormal bumps on the left side. "There's
a theory—granted, not proven, but generally accepted—
that offers cause for your impediment. In most males the
left side of the brain is dominant. It controls motor coordination, balance, and especially language abilities. I
think there's a small war going on in your head continually that tends to make life a little more difficult than

for the rest of us." I pictured tanks and planes streaking across my brain, fighting one another, the right side bombarding the left. I wondered how I might go about calling a truce.

He told me that normally the left side easily dominated the right, smoothly governing speech. But in my case the right side was perhaps more powerful than it was supposed to be, and the left had to exert energy to gain and maintain control over my cognitive abilities.

My nervous system, he also explained, which carried the brain's signals to the motor centers of my body, was being overworked trying to sort out the crossed signals it was getting. And if outside pressure were added, or a pressure-causing incident (such as a date), my nervous center would be flooded. My system would temporarily short out. The stuttering would begin. And the the greater the pressure, the more the stuttering.

That was just one of several theories, he told me. But he said that whatever the true cause of my problem, it was definitely a neurological mix-up located in the brain. Anytime I had a visual or hearing problem, or even a perceptual lag, there would be a slow-down in my reading ability.

> I PICTURED TANKS AND PLANES STREAKING ACROSS MY BRAIN, FIGHTING ONE ANOTHER.

I confirmed that my reading speed was painfully slow, while speech and even my football playing had been adversely affected.

"Jamie," he said. "The dyslexic person is no dummy. That you must always remember. But this slowness causes a problem: boredom." I was astonished that this man was telling me my life story before I even had a chance to say more than a paragraph to him. Dr. Travis continued: "If you're not challenged and pushed in the classroom, you will probably become restless. A bright mind having difficulty taking in elementary information from the written page is not a happy situation. Are you frustrated often?"

"Quite a bit," I complained. "In fact, more at myself than at my professors. It drives me nuts when I have to read most of my material and I keep falling asleep after two pages. Most folks don't realize how many ways there are to get information other than from books. I find that if I take good notes during lectures, especially from an organized professor, and try to outline the important points he wants me to get out of the course, well, that makes a world of difference. I do a great deal of skimming, looking for the key paragraph that sums up the important material. Unfortunately, there are times when I just have to buckle down and read the whole assignment, which takes me about three times as long as my classmates. Then my only aid is sheer discipline. But I'm so easily distracted that those sessions are the toughest. Finding a quiet place to read, keeping myself awake, outlining the important points—it's frustrating all right!"

Dr. Travis also asked me if I had noticed that most dyslexics were boys. "That's right! I only began noticing it recently. Why? I heard that boys don't do as well as girls during the early years in school. Maybe we're the weaker sex?" I joked.

"I wouldn't joke about being the weaker sex, if I were you," Dr. Travis said. He told me of studies that had been done showing that women take more pain than men, they generally they live longer, and at the fetal stage, they have fewer genetically caused problems. He said that male dyslexics account for about 80 percent of the total. (New research now shows an increase in females with learning disabilities; they simply hide it better.)

As I left Dr. Travis's office, my appetite was whetted for more information about the medical side of my disorder. The more I learned about it, the more I found my frustration and anger falling into place. In a magazine article, I found the answers to some of my questions. For instance, I learned that many dyslexics frequent museums and educational movies to compensate for their lack of book learning. I wondered how many times I had visited the Smithsonian Institution, trying to satisfy my curiosity about art, aerospace, and history after books failed to convey the knowledge. It was so much easier for me to take in information through actual contact with the piece to be studied or by listening to a lecture by a guide or narrator while I looked at the object. This kind of education opened a new world of information that books had never given to me. My ears were my greatest educational aids.

The magazine article also stated that many dyslexics end up in jail or in juvenile facilities. I could sympathize with them. There had been times when I wanted to give up the daily fight at school and at home, to stop working the extra hour or concentrating on simply keeping my voice from stuttering. At night I sometimes became depressed and let myself believe I was a dummy and would be stupid all my life. I would become convinced that it was only a matter of time before my friends discovered the truth and rejected me. At other times, depression would turn into anger as I blamed God and the world for what I had to deal with above and beyond the normal problems that life throws our way. Then the anger would surface as a violent fantasy.

My stereo thumped and boomed with the latest rock hits from the West Coast, its powerful amplifier drowning out

all other noises outside my room. I sat, my eyes fixed on
a blemish on the far wall, my mind traveling back away
from my room into a world of my own making.

All about me crouched my foul enemies, staring out
from the darkness, their greenish evil eyes gleaming in
the dusk. I stood alone—always in my fantasies I was the
loner—awaiting their attack. My automatic rifle was cradled in my sweating hands, the trigger finger of my right
hand at the ready. Slowly the largest of the hated enemy
began to move toward me, crouching as he advanced,
now no more than three hundred yards off, occasionally
taking cover behind one of the giant oaks that were scattered through the valley below me. He wore brown jack-
boots, their steel studs glittering in the moonlight. His
camouflage pants and tunic were crisscrossed with am-
munition belts and grenades. In his hand he gripped a
blue-steel-barreled automatic. I could not make out his face.
It was hidden under layers of dark greasepaint, but his flashing green eyes looked familiar.

Running up the hill toward my unprotected position,
he raised his gun to his shoulder and began firing, the
blue and red tracers of his fire drifting up in graceful arcs.
I had one chance: dashing to a boulder. I faltered and
fell writhing, in mock pain, finally lying still. My enemy
approached. He advanced and looked over my fallen
body with a grin of pride. He had hit his mark. With the
butt of his rifle he flipped my limp form over to see where
his bullets had penetrated. There was no blood to be
seen on me. Surprised, he stepped back, suspecting a
trap. It was too late. I rolled over and raised my weapon
and fired point-blank, the blast of my cartridges spewing
sparks over us both. He reeled and sank into the ground.

Quickly I took my bandanna from my head and wiped
the greasepaint and blood from his face. As the last of
the camouflage was removed from the sharp features, I
recognized the fallen form at my feet: it was the boy who

only a month ago had cruelly teased me about my stuttering. Satisfied, I stood and silently jogged into the forest.

I was startled from my daydream, feeling guilty over my fantasy. Did I really hate the boy who had teased me about my speech? Christians weren't supposed to allow themselves such thoughts. I quickly returned to my homework, burying the dream in the recesses of my mind. Why was I always having such violent fantasies? Was I some sick-o?

> **THERE HAD BEEN TIMES WHEN I WANTED . . . TO STOP WORKING THE EXTRA HOUR OR CONCENTRATING ON SIMPLY KEEPING MY VOICE FROM STUTTERING.**

The magazine article made sense out of those fantasies. Anger was by no means unusual for people with a handicap to fight. They were angry over the supposed injustice of it all and frustrated by their own failings. Here again discipline was needed. It was the cure-all for the learning disabled. I had to find healthy ways of dealing with the accumulated anger that was a by-product of my fight against a learning disability. Running until I almost dropped, lifting weights, hitting hard in football—all of them helped to express in a creative way frustration and anger that were and still are so prevalent in me.

A cute uniform-clad schoolgirl tapped me on my shoulder, rousing me from my thoughts. "Jamie, you've only got two minutes before you go onstage. I thought you might miss your call," she whispered shyly. Thanking her, I stood and stretched my legs. I could see Shirley preparing to go onstage. She played Jean Brodie with fire, and it was all I could do to keep her from dominating the scenes with her presence. The lights dimmed and I prepared to enter as Teddy Lloyd, the unfaithful art teacher whose principal aim in the show is to regain the love of Jean Brodie.

After that came tryouts for *Pericles*, and I got the lead. Chris was to take the narrator's role. Pulling me aside, Ted Walch explained that although Chris was the best actor our school had that year, I was given the part because of my height and presence. Ted Walch wanted to be sure that my success didn't give me a swelled head. *Pericles* meant that more work had to be squeezed into my schedule. Weekly voice sessions were coupled with daily memorization periods. I had six weeks to memorize hundreds of lines of Shakespeare, let alone staging and rehearsing their delivery with over sixty other actors who were to participate in the show. I was becoming very comfortable onstage. I relished being able to control my audience, knowing there was little chance of being rejected. At times it seemed that all my energies were being directed toward one goal: avoiding rejection.

CHAPTER 11

Complicated Feelings

The man facing me outweighed me by thirty pounds, and I was supposed to move him? The humid Ohio heat seeped into our sweat-soaked uniforms, making them sag and crimp uncomfortably. A stream of perspiration dripped down my nose and onto the dusty ground. A sharp bark came from the quarterback to my left; with the second "hut" I fired off into my opponent, trying to get my shoulder into his thighs and direct him away from our bruised running back. With the familiar crash of helmets, curses, and grunts, the College of Wooster football team practiced away the preseason summer. The men I was up against were mostly corn-fed boys who loved football and played like demons dedicated to their passion. I, on the other hand, had played the game for the fun of it. I was getting my first taste of the real thing in Ohio: These guys meant business. Fun wasn't in their vocabulary.

Being a green freshman, I was hoping that joining the football team would help me become accustomed to my new school, located in the middle of the northern Ohio cornfields. Better, I thought, to attack the new environment than whimper about it. I had no intention of being a typical "frosh." I wanted to get involved immediately in the life of my new world. Having moved from school to school so often, I figured that any new environment could be conquered by sheer energy and participation.

Glaring ahead through my face mask, I eyed the player opposite me. He had already embarrassed me twice in front of the coach. This time I was going to hit him a tad lower, attempting to knock him off his keel. I was running out of tricks and hoping this one would work. I knew the enemy in front of me; I had scrimmaged against him for two weeks, yet I had no awareness of the other enemy inside me. Dyslexia and hyperkinesia still had some fight left in them; although they had been soundly defeated on the academic field, they could still do plenty of damage in other areas of my life. With my confidence growing, I had thought very little about my learning disability during the past year. I hoped it was behind me, like acne, something to be outgrown and left with adolescence. I was soon to be proved wrong.

On the theater board was a sign-up sheet. Tryouts were being held for *Harvey*, and the theater was calling to me again. As I walked down the hall toward the Freedlander complex, a series of theaters and workshops donated to Wooster by a local merchant, I felt an urge to be back onstage. With football and freshman first quarter, not to mention an active Christian fellowship on campus, I was committed to the limit, yet the call was clear. Something about the lights and the audience awaiting the performance enthralled me, and although I was never much for the smell of greasepaint, I did long to be in front of a full house again. Turning the last corner, I entered the complex; red-carpeted and wood-paneled, the theater was magnificent. Up to that point Wooster had placed second to St. Albans by architectural standards, but the theater had St. Albans's beat hands down.

Light racks were cleverly hung from catwalks above my head. Busy technicians were fussing with the elevator that waited onstage, ready to transport the orchestra underground, out of sight of the audience. The four hundred plush seats, clustered between wide aisles, faced a stage area with good depth. *No more crowding backstage during a show,* I thought; I could hardly wait to try out. Why else was I here but to take advantage of all there was to participate in! Football was not enough of an extracurricular activity to stop me from acting, I decided. I added my name to the list and anxiously awaited the auditions.

My schedule was complete. I was picked for a middle-sized role in *Harvey,* which made my schedule one of the toughest I could have chosen. It wasn't unusual for me to spend two to three hours an afternoon cramming for my Greek class. Geology labs took two precious afternoons a week; I had football practice for three hours every weekday, with games on the weekends; Friday evening was given to church fellowship or acting rehearsal: all that in addition to three classes five days a week. But I thought I could handle it. I scheduled my time ruthlessly, often missing lunch to put more time in on the books. I avoided the library, which proved to be a social center. Rather, I hid in the theater building, studying in a deserted dressing room beneath the auditorium.

I HATED TO BE UNDER PRESSURE FOR A DEADLINE. IF I FINISHED EARLY, THEN I WAS IN CHARGE OF THE DEADLINE.

My desk faced a green wall at the far end of the chang-

ing room. The tile floor beneath me reflected the fluorescent ceiling light against the walls. I was in my private
shelter. I could be alone there to study and try to gain
control of my steadily increasing workload. Scattered ran-
domly on the desk were my flash cards: on one side was
the Greek word or ending to be memorized, on the other
was the meaning in English. My stack was ever growing
and now filled two boxes. How was I going to keep up
with it all? My wrist ached from the fall I had taken the
day before during football practice, but I could not stop
writing. A paper was due the next week in freshman studies class, and I wanted to finish early.

I hated to be under pressure for a deadline. If I finished
early, then *I* was in charge of the deadline. I had con-
trived a complex system to insulate me from pressure,
anxiety, loneliness, and lack of satisfaction. How could I
be lonely for intimate friendships when I was busy every
night of the week acting? No professor could add anxiety
to my life. I was far too disciplined for that and usually
had my assignments done a couple of weeks in advance.
How could I be discontented when my schedule was so
full of activities? I had built an unshakable foundation
for my life and was squeezing every drop out of the world
around me.

I was surrounded by rocks and specimens staring out at
me from cardboard boxes and cases. Books were strewn
everywhere, crammed into shelves haphazardly and
shoved under desks and tables. Thick dust covered the
upper shelves where strange geologic instruments peered
over the edges, hoping someday to return to their tasks.
Yellowing comics taped to file cabinets made passing
jokes about rocks and those who collected them. Amused
by the nearest one, I smiled, but quickly wiped the ex-

pression off my face, knowing full well that this was not an occasion for humor. I had only recently begun pulling my geology grade up to the level my professor, Dr. Cropp, thought I was capable of achieving. Dr. Cropp was now encouraging me to continue my efforts and pull it yet higher. I had to admire the man for pushing his students to do their best—too many teachers allowed their pupils to get by with good work when they were capable of doing better.

Settling back into his swivel chair, Dr. Cropp pointed with his thick, hairy arm toward the theater. "You're in that show, aren't you, what's its name, *Harold?*" he asked.

"Yeah, I'm in the show, but its name is *Harvey*. We only have two more weeks before it goes off, so we're pushing rehearsals fairly hard," I answered.

"Evans, with my class and the labs, football and then Greek—is that it? You're taking Greek, too?—well, with this play it adds up to about the busiest schedule I've seen in a freshman yet. You're trying to get your money's worth from this college, eh?" The man across the desk from me was all energy. In class he could hold the attention of sixty students, with both dramatic gestures and terror tactics. He continually pushed us to realize the value of geology, to appreciate the importance of the Jurassic Period and find it far more enticing than the sunny fall morning outside. Do well for his class and you received affirmation up to your armpits, but heaven help the student who was bright and did poorly. One of the famous Cropp notes was certain to appear in your mailbox if you disappointed him. I had received such a note telling me in no uncertain terms that I was to do better on the next test. I had no intention of receiving another.

Jogging down the creaking oak steps of the geo building, I headed toward the dorm. I was feeling good after my talk with Dr. Cropp, and a celebration was in order. There was no harm in skipping an hour's worth of studying.

As I passed the freshman women's dorm just in front of my own, I noticed a girl sitting on the steps. Hadn't I seen her at church fellowship? Yes, I had. In fact, I had asked her if she was a senior and was embarrassed to find out that she was a frosh, like me. Now she was sitting all alone on the steps of Holden Dorm, soaking up the last rays of the fall sun, her blue eyes flashing in the filtered light. A chill gust of wind blew the leaves from the huge oak above us into a rain of brown and yellow. Turning her blond head to avoid the shower of leaves, she glanced down, catching me staring at her. Embarrassed, I turned and headed toward my dorm. Then I stopped, remembering an old line someone had told me: "Life goes to those who grab it." The advice seemed appropriate to the moment. Turning around, I headed for the steps and invited the girl to have dinner with me that evening. I felt terribly bold at the time and managed to get the invitation out without many stutters or slurs.

The dinner led to a date that Friday evening after play rehearsal, which in turn led to a movie the next weekend. Soon I found myself engrossed in a relationship with a charming person. Until that time at Wooster I had been obediently following a monk's life of hard work and exercise, but such disciplined habits could give me only a marginal satisfaction. They could hardly satisfy a hungry heart. In Angela I found sensitivity and depth, attributes my Greek primer and stage life could not offer.

Angela's room was on the third floor of Holden Dorm, which was locked to male visitors after eleven o'clock on weeknights. Unfortunately my play rehearsals were not over until at least eleven-thirty. Obviously we had a problem. How were two romantically inclined freshmen to spend time together when one was scheduled solid until eleven-thirty and the other was locked away at eleven?

Staring at the ice-covered rung about three feet from my outstretched arm, I was struck with an idea. The fire escape led right past Angela's window; if I could jump to the first rung of the elevated ladder I could haul myself up and climb to her room. She might—with luck—be in, and in the darkness I had a good chance of making it without being nailed by the campus security guards.

The snow squeaked under my feet as I prepared to jump. With a final glance to check for passersby, I vaulted up. Grabbing the iced-over rung, I hauled myself up, hanging momentarily upside down, imagining the newspaper headline: "Wooster Boy Shot Trying to Force Way Into Coed Dorm." I slipped and held on to the icy rail. The old fire escape creaked loudly under my weight. I began to ascend the steps, praying they would hold. As I passed a second-floor room, a window shade suddenly whipped shut, scaring me to the point of almost falling off the step. I jumped to the wall, pinning myself against its icy stonework. No one appeared at the window; still I waited. I had no desire to be hauled up in front of the judicial board for being a peeping Tom.

Crouching and crawling to the next level, I tapped on Angela's window with half-frozen hands. Why had I forgotten my gloves? I looked behind me down into the street, watching for the security patrol's headlights. Finally Angela opened her window. She was startled but invited me in, and that was the first of many post-practice hours we spent together. When it was time for me to leave, I would creep down the fire escape and steal into my dorm a few feet away. I was beginning to care for Angela more and more. She was beautiful, yes, but there was more to her. I was attracted every bit as much by her intelligence, her faith, and her delightful wit.

Six weeks later, as I was preparing to depart her room after an evening when the talk had been warm and good, I was stopped dead in my tracks. Something was very wrong. A slow dread was coming over me; I wanted out of the room, now barely lit by a single candle flickering on a makeshift table made from a trunk, the Detroit airport stickers visible under a lace cover. Feeling a little sick to my stomach, I recalled the evening's events. Had we done anything to be ashamed of? No, there was no cause for guilt. I turned to look at Angela, who was in front of a mirror on the trunk. The softness of her hair was practically irresistible, and I would always mess it up. Catching my expression in the mirror, she turned and put down her comb.

"You look as if you just ate a frog that didn't quite agree with you, mister. Got something on your mind you want to talk about?" she asked. I winced at the question. It made me feel as if she were looking directly into my heart. Attempting to regain control of the situation, I smiled and kissed her goodnight. But the sick feeling inside me was growing.

"No, just a mood. It'll pass," I said as I put on my jacket, pulling the leather gloves from my pockets. (I had learned that leather was much better than skin against frozen fire escape bars.)

"You sure you're feeling all right?" she probed. Putting my leg out the window, I gave her a wink.

"You didn't answer my question, Jamie," she called after me as I hit the snow beneath the fire escape.

"Really, Angela, I feel fine. I just need some sleep," I lied as I turned toward my dorm and jogged to the door.

I lay awake staring out my window into the cold Ohio night. A light snow was falling, adding to the three inches we had received two days earlier. I had finally identified the sick feeling: I was anxious. I felt trapped in the relationship. My attraction for Angela was fading fast, although I was deeply drawn to everything I had learned about her. So why did I want to run? She certainly hadn't put any pressure on me to intensify the relationship, nor had she been anything but supportive and affirming. The answer must be inside me, yet I couldn't find it no matter how many times I examined my feelings. I simply wanted out.

I awoke after a restless night to find a wonderland of snow covering the campus. And the dread was still there. My head was pounding, and I knew I had to get out of the relationship. Only my conscience kept me from going over to Angela's room and breaking the news that very minute.

"Wait; you've got to wait—it'll pass, the attraction will come back," I told myself as I shaved in the steamy bathroom, stopping to wipe the mirror free of the mist. I tried to believe it was a bad dream and made up my mind that I was going to out-last any crazy urge to run away from Angela when things with her couldn't be better.

At breakfast my normally stacked tray was empty that morning. I could stomach only orange juice. Then I tried to get relief from my thoughts by attacking my Greek assign-

I HAD FINALLY IDENTIFIED THE SICK FEELING: I WAS ANXIOUS. I FELT TRAPPED IN THE RELATIONSHIP.

ment. For about an hour I forgot about my urge to leave Angela, but it returned even more violently when I tried to eat lunch. The full glass of milk shivered slightly as my hand tensed: Angela had just entered the dining room and I started looking for the nearest exit. What was with me?

After a week of constant pressure, I made up my mind. I couldn't fake what I didn't feel any longer. I had to call it quits with her, although I could find no good reason for it.

She was in the laundry room folding the last of a load

of clothes when I found her. One look at my face and she knew what was coming, yet she took it well. "Look, we're too young to be getting serious," I told her, rationalizing, although we were in no danger of becoming serious; we had been careful.

She was too good a sport to argue. She accepted my explanation, although it was shot full of holes. With a smile, she agreed that we should work on being friends. I nodded, feeling like a liar. I had no desire to be friends. Even that I would have to fake if I was to avoid hurting her. What was wrong with me? I had never been in such a state of flight from a relationship before. Why didn't I even want to have a friendship with someone who only a week earlier was the closest friend I had at Wooster? As I left the laundry room, I looked back at Angela. Her face was set in a friendly good-bye, yet her eyes described her real feelings. They were dulled by the hurt that was welling up inside her. I didn't want to see her cry, so I went to get my running gear.

Running alone through the snow-covered fields behind our school did much to ease my mind. It made my muscles ache so much that I lost my need to feel guilty over Angela. In fact, I felt wonderful for a time, relishing my regained independence and the ability to give 100 percent to my work. But within a week my heart was hungry again. I was not satisfied in my discipline-controlled world. I had no intimacy in my life and at night I longed to be able to open my mind to someone who understood. But the fear of having that urge to flee kept me in my firmly fixed schedule and I allowed no one to enter it as Angela had done. I was hoping that the breakup was a typically adolescent occurrence. Unfortunately, I would eventually learn that the motivations underlying it were far from typical.

It was summer, and I was grateful to leave Wooster and head for California, where I had a job as a camp counselor for the summer. I needed a change. I also was looking forward to working with Jim Slevcove; I had heard he was a special kind of person.

Climbing the pine steps to the Slevcoves' mountain home, we prepared to begin our weekly staff meeting. It was normal policy at Yosemite Sierra Summer Camp to discuss each child who would be attending the coming three-week session. Jim Slevcove, the camp owner, believed personal attention was the key to a camper's growth, and he pushed his staff to understand their kids. Sipping our mugs of apple cider and tea, we gathered around a comfortable living room, our ranks bulging into the halls. Over 120 children ranging in age from eight to fifteen were to be reviewed that night.

With a Russian pastry balanced on his lap and a folder in his hand, Slevcove swallowed the last of his tea and paused. We were midway through our session; only sixty more new arrivals to go. Outside, one of the maintenance trucks purred by in the cool evening, momentarily quieting the chirp of crickets and the rustle of pine needles in the dry breeze.

"Vince, this is a special case," Jim began, calling across the room to the bearded giant who was to head one of the younger groups. Holding the folder at arm's length, attempting to focus on the print, the middle-aged Russian continued: "Paul is a hyperactive child, Vince—to an extreme degree."

At that my ears tingled. So here was a kid with my problem.

"He's been a discipline problem at home and school but has a loving father who frankly is at a loss as to how to control the boy's energy. The mother died two years ago."

I winced at the news. Hyperactivity is hard enough to deal with when there are two loving parents in the home.

But a single-parent situation . . . How was the father coping?

"Paul may need more attention than the other boys in your cabin, so be forewarned. Firmness and discipline are recommended, but priority number one is love," Jim concluded.

May need more attention, I thought to myself. Now that was an understatement. Vince was in for an experience, and I wanted to be close enough to watch.

The bus from L.A. arrived and discharged its cargo of energetic youth. Keeping an eye out for Paul as I welcomed my own cabin kids, I wondered if I was going to be seeing a copy of myself during my early years. I saw him that evening when the whole camp was gathered together.

Vince's face was already scarlet. Seven of the eight boys in his cabin were neatly seated along the paneled wall, as Vince had instructed; the eighth, a sturdy little guy in blue shorts and sneakers, was investigating the spotlight fixture above the window, not bothering to listen to his counselor's objections. As the meeting proceeded, Vince repeatedly had to rebuke Paul, to their mutual embarrassment, while Paul busily carried on his investigation, distracting the other boys with his activity. Intently watching an ant as it crawled across the worn rug, Paul would suddenly turn back to examine his neighbor's shoelace. The boy was in perpetual motion. He was on Ritalin, too, and it wasn't slowing him down much.

By the end of a week, Vince was on the edge of insanity. All his attempts to discipline the child into obedience had been fruitless. Paul was the bad boy of the camp, always into mischief, constantly seeking attention through malicious actions. He was crying out for help, that was clear enough, and his antisocial habits only mirrored his image of himself. Bad boys do bad things, so he was doing his best to play the role. *Could the rejection that his hyperactivity had brought down upon him have caused all this?* I asked myself.

As I realized how similar we were, an idea struck me. If I were Paul, I speculated, what would I want most during our evening meetings? Why would I always be moving around? Getting attention didn't seem to be the answer.

At our next group gathering, when Paul began to raise his usual ruckus, I called him over to sit with me. Reluctantly he agreed. As the evening talk began, 119 children gave their attention to the speaker, an engrossing six-foot-eight basketball player who had devoted his life to Christian ministry—but Paul followed the flight of a moth fluttering in the window, the soft purr of its wings distracting him. Grabbing him by the waist, I hoisted him into my lap and began rubbing his back. Amazed, Vince watched as Paul settled down, listening placidly to the speaker, moving

I WAS NOT SATISFIED IN MY DISCIPLINE-CONTROLLED WORLD.

only to ask me an occasional question. After that night whenever a speaker would begin to talk, I was sure to find Paul demanding to climb up on my lap for a back rub, and as long as the rub lasted, so did his attention to the evening's message.

There was nothing special about my backrubs. I was simply meeting Paul's need for activity. As long as his nervous system was being stimulated, even from an outside source, he was able to calm down. When there was no outside stimulation, his disability forced him to initiate it himself through his activity. Like Paul, I found it far easier to concentrate when I was moving. Sitting still requires energy that ideally should be used to retain information. But if I can answer my nervous system's need for activity, then I can concentrate.

The fall of my sophomore year at Wooster found me in rare high spirits. The summer in Yosemite had been good for me. I had made some new friends and enjoyed the company of a fine woman who made me feel on top of the world. But it wasn't long before I was once more caught up in an impossibly crowded schedule, which began to take its toll. I was driving myself ruthlessly, trying to ignore that old hungry feeling in my heart.

Memories of Angela made me reluctant to get seriously involved with another woman. What would happen if the urge to run away came out of nowhere and wrecked another seemingly healthy relationship?

I was sitting with my back to the main entrance of the dining room one day, stuffing the last forkful of spaghetti into my already overcrowded mouth. As usual I had eaten more than a human being had a right to eat, and the familiar stretching of my stomach was becoming a wonderful ritual. Wooster's food was too good. Opposite me, my buddy Don eyed the women students. He didn't see the girl coming up behind us, but when she stopped and said hello to him, I saw why he suddenly ran out of jokes. She was the epitome of health and vivaciousness, and her deep-green eyes sparkled as she said no. She couldn't join us because she was sitting with someone else. She pointed to a mustached senior who was reserving a table for them in the far corner of the dining room. She thanked Don for the invitation and left.

"Darned seniors," Don grumbled, "always snatching the best women before we underclassmen even have a chance. Think we could arrange an accident for him, maybe a meeting with the town bus, head on at fifty miles an hour?" he fantasized.

"Don, what did you say her name was?" I asked.

"She's one of the Morgan kids. There's a whole bunch

of them here. Her dad's a contractor in Philadelphia. Her name's Melanie . . . Melanie Morgan. Fine, ain't she?"

I agreed. "Is she really dating this senior dude? I mean, are they serious?" I asked.

"I thought you swore off women for the duration?" Don teased. "You must be nuts, Evans. You're out to lunch if you think she'll go with you over a senior. But, wait, there may be hope yet—from what I hear, they're almost on the rocks. You may have your chance."

We were preparing for midterm, and the play rehearsal schedule was increasing. I forgot about Melanie Morgan because I had so many other things to keep me busy. Busy, yes, but not really happy.

With the spring quarter came news from Don that Melanie and her senior friend had split up, meaning she was probably free to be asked out. I had no trouble remembering who she was. Don was smart enough to let the seed of his announcement grow in my mind, figuring I'd act soon enough.

That afternoon I had an appointment with my religion professor. On my way to his house I was struck with the realization that for too long I had sat back and allowed valuable relationships to slip by. Melanie was too much of an attraction to pass up now that she was free, and having decided that, I rang the Bairds' doorbell. I was greeted by Mary Baird, who supplied the doctor and me with ample sandwiches and tea as we launched into a theological discussion. Dr. Baird opened his home to many of the students within the Religion Department, using it as an off-campus classroom in which he took us deeper into the intricacies of religious thought than he could do in a formal class setting.

I was distracted that day, though, and missed an obvious point I should have grasped easily. Dr. Baird understood. "Don't blame you in the least, Jamie, for having your mind on other things than Tillich and Harnack," he said. "At your age on a fine day like this, I would have been hard pressed to keep my wits about me. Anyone in particular, son?"

"Not yet, sir," I answered.

"Well, the 'yet' seems promising. Yes, a balance is necessary for any healthy theologian, Jamie. Never dedicate your life to books, son. Relationships are the meat of life; books are only guides to the important things. Serving Christ, living with a woman like my wife, Mary—they really matter. Do you know that Mary's my toughest critic and greatest asset? Couldn't publish one of my books without her. Academics . . . they're not the end, they're simply the means to a higher end."

I was surprised by his advice. Although I could never be accused of dedicating my life to books, my schedule certainly had become king during the past two years, and production meant more to me than relationships. Had I gone wrong somewhere? Was I *too* disciplined?

> **I WAS STRUCK WITH THE REALIZATION THAT FOR TOO LONG I HAD SAT BACK AND ALLOWED VALUABLE RELATIONSHIPS TO SLIP BY.**

Walking back from the Bairds', I passed a group of Frisbee-throwing friends, running in the sun and grabbing the flying disk with all their energy. Jogging on to my room, I pulled on my running gear and headed toward Melanie's dorm. Maybe she'd be outside in the quad, sunning. I could sneak into her dorm and leave a note asking her to dinner.

I was crouching by her message board writing the invitation when the door opened and she entered. Ignoring my embarrassment, she greeted me with a smile that made me realize I had chosen the right day to visit. She, too, was clad in running clothes and shoes, and within minutes we found ourselves jogging easily toward Miller's Pond Park, talking lightly about the day's activities and our interests. By the end of our run I knew I was in trouble. My days of total dedication to my schedule were numbered. Here was a person who had the ability to attract me intellectually, physically, and spiritually—a triple threat if I ever saw one. Jogging was just the beginning. Our dinner conversations ran into the early evening, making me repeatedly late for rehearsal. Communication had never been so good, and I relished the hours we spent exploring one another's lives.

Outside, the moon was peeping over the horizon, resembling a trimmed fingernail. A light spring breeze wafted through the porch as we sat comfortably tucked away in a far corner of the college houses. The campus was quiet, the last of the blasting stereos silenced as the beer ran out at the fraternity parties. Couples strolled by, heading for their dorms, not noticing the two figures sitting close in the shadowed shelter of the porch. "Jamie, what are you thinking about? You've been quiet for a while," Melanie said.

I had been feeling angry toward my family, toward my brothers in particular, and was not sure why. Hesitantly I began. "I'm wondering why I didn't get a whole lot of time with my brothers as a kid. We didn't see much of each other. Every now and then I get real mad at them for that and it scares me. I mean, you're not supposed to be mad at your family, and that was a long time ago. So why am I mad now?"

Across the street the last lights flicked off in a nearby house. Wooster was beginning to resemble a ghost town. A warm hand found mine as Melanie said: "I think it's normal to be angry with your brothers and sister. I am, all the time. Sometimes I could wring my little brother's neck."

"But, Melanie, I'm angry over things that went down eight years ago. That's weird," I continued. I wondered if the spider spinning its web to my left had any designs on making a home out of my jacket, hung on the rail next to it. Melanie thought the streetlights made the web look like a mass of silver threads giving off white energy. She had an eye for natural wonders.

I HAD NEVER ADMITTED MY ANGER TO ANYONE BEFORE AND FELT A LITTLE NAKED AFTER TELLING HER ABOUT IT.

I had never admitted my anger to anyone before and felt a little naked after telling her about it. Yet there was an exhilaration too. It seemed as if she really wanted to hear about it. Stealing a bobby pin from her sun-streaked hair, I began to bend it into a spring as she asked: "You haven't talked about this much, have you? Private about a lot of things, right? You and your independent ways. What are you afraid of?" She was whispering as she snuggled closer. "Are you afraid I'll run off with all your secrets and discover you're human, like the rest of us?" she asked. Turning my head to take on her question, I received a big kiss on the nose. Winking, she pulled my ear and said she was only teasing.

"Mr. Evans, I like you," she added.

"The feeling's mutual, Ms. Morgan." A long silence followed. I had never before communicated with anyone on such an intimate level.

I looked at the applications on the bed in front of me. Wooster offered programs off campus, and the two I was considering were for Scotland and Arizona, a total of ten months away from Ohio. Eyeing the parking lot outside my room, I watched an old Buick struggling to get started in the winter cold. Its battery had obviously frozen, depleting at least half its power. "That car would have a hard time running in perfect weather, let alone fifteen below," I grumbled to myself, returning my easily distracted attention to the application forms. The Ohio winter was wearing on me. I needed a change of pace from institutional living, and the off-campus programs seemed to be just the ticket. Getting credit for traveling abroad was too good to pass up. Or was something else making me want to leave Wooster? Was I getting too serious about Melanie? We had been going together for four months, which was certainly no record, yet she had probed deeper into my life than anyone else.

Taking my well-worn diary from the shelf beside my ancient desk, I skimmed through the entries, smiling at the inscription that Melanie had made on the cover the day she gave me the blank book. Scanning through its contents, I noticed that she was a regular topic of my writing. I read the entry for October 12, three months earlier: "It's late, just returned from Melanie's room. What a talk we had! Mostly about God and how the campus is lacking fellowship, but also about family matters. Seems Melanie comes from a pretty well put together home. She's continually digging into my background. Pretty soon she'll know all there is to know about me."

I thought back to the numerous other occasions when we had stayed up talking or just being together until late. They were fine recollections. Yet something within me wasn't feeling right. Was she part of the reason I wanted to get off campus for ten months? Dodging the question, I plunged into the application forms, throwing the diary into the corner. It was useless trying to sort out all my emotions and motivations. If I was to go, I'd know soon enough. Winding the first application into my ancient typewriter, I banged away at the necessary details, excited to be heading—I hoped—to Britain, where my brothers had been born.

The Arizona clay stuck to my boots as I struggled to settle the horse I was attempting to saddle. Our Wooster group, thirteen in all, were mounting up for a seven-hour ride through one of the many painted canyons of the Navajos. Anxiously I waited until the last of our group got into their saddles and we headed upstream on a rainy, cool morning. It was wonderful being back on a horse after so many weeks. The speckled gelding I was riding chafed at the bit uncomfortably seated in his mouth. He was eager for a run and let me know it by tugging continually at the reins, forcing me to hold him up again and again.

We approached the mouth of the canyon that was closed to all non-Native Americans without Navajo guides. Glancing back, I noticed that my friend Mark and I were beginning to outdistance our lead guide. I could see the cross look on the Navajo's face as we galloped away up the stream which, at times, flowed within inches of our stirruped boots. We had no intention of sticking with the slowest of our straggling group. We had riding to do and each of us was trying to outdo the other in speed and grace on our steeds. Splashing through a shallow channel, spray flying at our faces, we headed into the canyon proper, its red sandstone walls towering hundreds of feet above us. Our objective was the ruins of Cliff Dwellers, who had inhabited the region centuries ago. For some reason my mind went back to the day, months ago, when Melanie tried to teach me the proper way to ride a horse. She had a natural affinity for the beasts and easily put the biggest of her family's stock through its paces.

I thought of Melanie often, missing her very much as our group traveled through the Navajo reservation, studying its history and culture. I had been away from Wooster for two months, with eight more to go.

"You're thinking about Morgan again, aren't you, Evans?" Mark asked, breaking into my daydream.

Wiping the river water from my eyes, I nodded. "Really miss that woman, Mark. She's not leaving this boy's memory too easily."

Mark Rutledge knew me well enough to guess what was going through my mind. "Wonder if she'll wait for you to get back?" he thought aloud. "You'll be gone almost a year. Quite a test for even the best romance . . . Here comes that guide again; we'd better pick up the pace if we don't want to get shoved back with the rest of the group." With that, we kicked our mounts up to a respectable gallop and stormed through the next ford to the far bank, just out of earshot of our now exasperated guide.

I hope she'll wait, I thought to myself. I hadn't ever felt that way about a woman, and I was surprised that I was so willing to be committed to her. Maybe my motivation for leaving Wooster was simply that I had to get away from school and into a new environment for a respite. Maybe I wasn't running from Melanie, after all. Loosening the reins, I allowed my horse to gallop ahead of Mark's and dared him with a shout to a race. "We'll see what you're really made of, Rut! Try and keep up with me now, Skinny!" I taunted as we raced through one of

God's own masterpieces of natural splendor. I was in fine spirits, convinced that this time there would be no running away as there had been with Angela.

"Old Reeky," for the most part, stands on what used to be a bog, dominated by a volcanic plug that towers above it. On that rock jutting over the swamp, ingenious builders constructed a castle to defend the planned city below. Through the centuries the town grew, surrounding the castle and spreading to the sea's nearest inlet.

As I began my second program of study abroad in Scotland, I boarded a red double-decker bus for the twenty-minute ride to my school. I was attending New College, the University of Edinburgh's seminary, located in the shadow of the old castle. Cruising to school every morning by bus afforded me ample time to think and compose the letters I would write that evening to friends and family. Melanie was my most frequent correspondent, and as usual she drifted through my mind as I passed by the first of two train stations on the way to the university. Lately she had been on my mind almost nonstop, although I was four thousand miles and some months away from her and Ohio. Glancing at my watch, I attempted to estimate where she would be. "Seven A.M. here, 1 A.M. back in Wooster. She'll be settling in for the night after a long day of classes," I said to myself. I longed for her to be with me in Edinburgh exploring a new world together. Scotland was a wonderland of dilapidated castles, rich history, and bone-chilling winds. Many times I regretted Melanie's absence as I traveled the Highlands by train and foot that October; my only consolation was the letters we regularly sent to each other, filled with our thoughts and intimacies. But the written word couldn't convey the scent of the brewer's yeast that pervaded the old city or the sting of the morning mist as it hovered over the crags along the Highlands. No letter could warm a cold Scottish evening, either; paper wasn't meant for that sort of thing.

With a jolt, the bus turned the last roundabout curve and negotiated Prince's Street. Stumbling down the circular stairway that led to the bus's exit, I silently cursed the engineer who had designed these machines for people under six feet tall. I rubbed my bruised head, grateful to be out of the smoke-filled vehicle. Did everyone smoke in Scotland? I strode along the crowded sidewalk, climbed the hill to the coal-smoke-blackened university, and began my day's studies.

Between classes I headed for the small chapel below our library, where I was to meet Terry Gillespie, a fellow Wooster student who had also journeyed to Scotland to study theology. On Tuesday and Thursday afternoons we met in the tiny chapel to talk and pray, supporting each other as fellow foreigners. I was amazed, and more than a little thankful, at the way God had supplied such rich fellowship in both Arizona and Scotland. In the Navajo country Mark Rutledge had been a sounding board and a sensitive prayer partner. Now, here in Scotland, I had a new and spiritually mature companion in Terry. At the time, I didn't realize what God was building in those two men and how vital Mark and Terry were to be in the difficult and painful days to come. For the time being it was enough for me to have them as friends.

I was as satisfied as I had ever been with the schedule I had set for myself in Edinburgh. Finding the university's demands comparatively light, I was free to join the school's crew and lifting organizations, which were the equivalent of our American varsity sports programs. Although the crew and lifting teams lacked professionally trained coaches, we still worked hard. I took great delight in leaving my books by three in the afternoon. Already it was getting dark in that northern land as I trooped off to the gym facilities in a converted old brewery. There, for two glorious hours, I would be free to lift weights with a few fellow enthusiasts. Then I would run the length of Arthur's Seat, a nearby mountain, and jog over to the nearest bus stop, where I would catch a ride to our crew shack. Meeting my team in the adjacent pub, I'd down a warming drink with them to ward off the chilling cold, and then we'd all clamber into our boats. Never before had I found such an agreeable sport. The feeling of all four of us catching our oars in the water at the same moment, pulling with all our might, sending our feather-light craft zipping across the still canal water, was almost too much for me. There were no left or right signals to confuse me—only endurance, balance, and timing mat-tered. Dyslexia could do no harm.

I wasn't reluctant to leave Edinburgh. Though I en-joyed my independent schedule there, it was time to get back to Wooster, to my theological studies with Dr. Baird, and to Melanie. I was convinced that I was in love with her and was anxious to move our relationship forward. Barely making my connections from London to Dulles International, I was soon driving my ancient Toyota toward Wooster for the winter term of my junior year. Melanie was waiting for me. She had waited patiently for over ten months. As I crossed the ice-covered highways of Ohio, memories of my times with Melanie flooded my mind. Hadn't I left her during the winter? Now I was coming back with the snow that had sent me off.

I had arranged to meet her at her uncle's home just south of town where she would often spend the week-ends, avoiding the noisy parties that flourished during the winter months. Melanie wasn't a partygoer. She loved the quiet of the farm where she could snuggle by a fire with a book. Perhaps it was that serenity that so attracted me to her.

Turning the last corner of her uncle's long drive, I caught sight of her, pretty and green-eyed, nearly smothered in her winter coat and scarf, waving as I approached. A squadron of butterflies roared across my stomach as I guided the car through the deep snow and parked. How were we going to feel about each other now that we were face to face again instead of writing from the safety of four thousand miles? Would we be able to communicate the same vulnerability we had written in our letters, the same affection and hopes?

The weekend put my fears to rest. The two days Melanie and I spent together at the farm helping her uncle haul the winter's feed and doing odd chores were filled with easy talk and much affection. A gentle peace came over me, and the anxiety I had felt ten months earlier was gone. I was convinced that my restlessness during that time was a result of my heavy schedule and not my relationship with Melanie.

With a flurry of activity Wooster's winter term began. Classes, athletics, and fellowship demanded vast amounts of time, and by the first week of February I was again burning the candle at both ends. I was grateful for the discipline that dyslexia had demanded because it was paying off in classwork. I saw to it, however, that there was always time in the evenings for Melanie. She had a way of talking to me that eased my mind, and I found it easy to open up with her. Vulnerability had never come so naturally.

Curling up by the fire glowing in the giant stone hearth of Melanie's uncle's farm, we stared into the dying flames. We were there because one of the horses had slipped and required a trip to the vet, where it could be slung in a giant hammock while its shattered leg healed. Melanie's uncle had called us out to aid in the transportation of the animal, and both of us were only too glad to leave our books for a few days.

The wind screamed with an eerie wail, rattling the shutters on their rusted hinges. Staring at the snow drifting by the windowsill, I was hoping for at least six more inches. Kicking off my snow-soaked boots, I warmed my nearly frozen toes by the fire, as Melanie put away her latest book and settled by my side. "Do you still think much about your brothers?" she whispered, not wanting to wake her uncle, who was snoring in the next room. "You had a lot of anger surfacing before you left last year."

"I didn't think about it much in Scotland, but I guess it's still there," I replied slowly. "It's not only against my brothers, Melanie, there are others, too. Sometimes I just get mad and depressed for no apparent reason. Then the violent fantasies start up again and for about two or three days I'm pretty bad company." I had been running my hand through her hair and I stopped talking long enough to try to undo a tangle.

"Ouch!" she protested. "It hurts when you pull it out by the roots. Here. See how it feels?" Teasingly she pulled a single brown hair from my short-cropped mass of bristle.

A few moments of silence passed as I tossed a new log on the fire. "In Edinburgh I had a lot of violent thoughts," I said cautiously.

Melanie tossed her long blond hair behind her, keeping it out of my reach. While I had been away she had let it grow, and it was almost to the middle of her back. "So what's this about violent thoughts, Jamie? What's a violent thought?" she said. "Do your thoughts go around hitting people?" she joked.

"Very funny," I said, annoyed by the humor. "I get mad easily, but I hate to yell and make a scene, so when I get mad I just leave the room. That's when the violent thoughts begin. I'll think about doing the cruelest things to the person I'm mad at, but I'll never tell anybody I'm mad. Sometimes I dream about blowing away cars and people with a gun. Not that I'd ever do it, but I don't like thinking those things." We talked for hours while the snow fell outside. Then Melanie stretched and rose. She kissed me goodnight and headed for her room. Both of us were thoroughly talked out.

I leaned back against the couch, watching the last coals dying in the hearth. I had never told anyone before of my fantasies, and I felt funny about it. From deep within, a long-forgotten feeling crept up to my heart from my bowels. Wincing, I tried to identify it. I broke into a cold sweat, the back of my neck burning with anxiety. It was the way I had felt about Angela a few years earlier. I wanted to run. Intimacy was making me lose control, and I wanted out. My conscience quickly closed the door on my fear, pushing it back down whence it had come. Relaxing a little, I rose and went to my room. I was very tired. I went to bed hoping never to feel those old fears again. I still felt guilty about hurting Angela, and I didn't want to do anything like that again. Certainly not to Melanie.

> I WAS GRATEFUL FOR THE DISCIPLINE THAT DYSLEXIA HAD DEMANDED BECAUSE IT WAS PAYING OFF IN CLASSWORK.

CHAPTER 12

The One Opponent I'd Never Identified

My hand trembled as I opened the door to Melanie's dorm. It had been two weeks since we returned from her uncle's farm—two weeks of hell. I was in a constant struggle with myself: my conscience telling me to wait and pray, assuring me that the joy of the relationship would return, and an unexplainable fear urging me to run. I was out of control and could no longer dictate my life from hour to hour.

Each morning I woke up sick with turbulent emotions. Was I living a lie by going out with Melanie? Was I just using her companionship? Could I ever really commit myself to her? To anyone? My anxiety had destroyed my feeling for her, but I could see that she still felt the same toward me, and that only intensified my guilt. There was nothing we had done morally to feel guilty about, but we were as committed as I had ever been. What was happening to me? Was I unable to handle a relationship? I had never been so tortured by my own confusion.

The night before, she had looked straight into my eyes, and I felt as if she could see into my soul. I didn't have to say a word; she knew. Tears welled up in her green eyes and her lower lip trembled. I felt as if I had shot a young doe at point-blank range after masquerading as a game warden. Her expression kept me awake all night. *Was that the way I rewarded someone who loved me so unselfishly?* I wondered, and my conscience was quick to condemn me.

Retreating from the door, I sat down on the steps. What could I say to make things better? How could I apologize? How could I explain what I myself didn't understand? Again my conscience pummeled me, telling me to stop being a coward and work on the relationship. But it was no use; I was ruled by my fears. I walked out onto the snow-filled field, heading for nowhere. I was tired. My head ached, the pain coming from the back of my neck and stretching across to my forehead. Was I incapable of love? The thought frightened me. Why did I feel so tired? It was over between us. It was my fault and that was that. Changing course, I headed back toward my dorm. I wanted to sleep, to find some respite from the war going on inside me.

Waking at dawn, I stumbled into the bathroom, feeling more tired than I had the night before. The cool shower running over me could not reduce the burning sensation that crisscrossed the back of my neck. As I walked to class in the chill of morning, my mind struggled to make sense of it all. Looking up, I saw Melanie coming down the same walkway, talking with one of her friends. Avoiding their glances, I headed across the grass, taking a shortcut to class. My conscience accused me: "Coward, you're avoiding her! You can't even face her. You're a sick boy!"

Class was no better. My mind would not obey my commands. It would wander restlessly from the memory of Melanie's face to my conviction that I was a coward who could not love but could only hurt. In my clearer moments I considered that the breakup with Melanie was not a problem but rather the symptom of something deeper brewing within me, yearning to get out. But those moments were very few, and the rest of the time I spent tearing myself apart, eating into what little self-esteem I had left. My weight dropped significantly. I was lethargic and abandoned my usual schedule of running and lifting. I stopped going to church fellowship meetings. Discipline, my main strength, had slipped through my fingers.

I fumbled with the card in front of me. On it was a phone number provided by the college operator. It was the number of the school psychologist, Betty Schull. I wanted to end the nightmare I had been living in. I wanted to end it so badly that I was willing to swallow what pride I had left and seek a professional's help. Picking up the phone, I dialed. I saw visions of burly men in white suits coming with straitjackets to haul me off to the mental ward. It didn't matter. I was so tired of the war going on within me that anything would have been better.

The voice on the other end of the phone was a warm one. Yes, it would be all right if I came over to talk. Would three o'clock tomorrow be convenient? Hanging up the phone, I shuffled down the hall to my room, feeling no better than before I dialed.

The next day I gripped my yellow legal pad as I nervously waited for the three o'clock appointment. I prayed that no one would ask me why I had come to the student health center. "Are you sick? Do you have the flu?" How was I supposed to answer their questions? *No, I don't have the flu. I'm just fighting a losing battle with my brain and feel like giving up. I'm ripping myself apart at the seams because I think I'm going mad. You know—a mental case, a nut!* Fortunately, no one came in while I was waiting for Betty Schull to see me. No one asked any embarrassing questions. Taking a seat in a comfortable-looking stuffed chair, she asked me to use the couch. I groaned. I could just see myself lying on some shrink's couch! Perceiving my hesitation, she intervened. "Most people just sit on it, Jamie—no need to be anything here but comfortable." Relieved, I sat down and faced the woman who resembled my mother more than she did a doctor. "So, what can I do for you?" she asked.

Diving right in, I read what I had written on my legal pad. I wanted to be sure not to miss a thing, so I had listed all the feelings and ideas that seemed related to my problem. After listening to me read for forty-five minutes, she interrupted. "I think you were right about that last point, Jamie."

Consulting my list, I said, "You mean the thing about the breakup with Melanie being a symptom, not the cause of it all?"

She nodded and told me to put down the pad. She had heard me read enough. "In my experience, Jamie, it isn't unusual for a person to take a full year to get over a broken relationship. It's only natural for both parties to be hurt. The one who was dropped will suffer some lack of self-worth and feel he or she didn't measure up to the needs of the other. I expect that Melanie will be feeling that way, and there is nothing you can do about it, even though you say it was not her fault. Leave her alone until she's ready to initiate communication. This is a hard rule, but I believe in it. The one who is rejected is the one who should decide when and if there is to be a friendship between the two. As for you, you said there was nothing you could have done but break things off. In that case, your guilt is ridiculous. If there was nothing else you could have done, why do you feel guilty?"

I couldn't answer her question, and sat silently.

I began seeing Dr. Schull twice a week. We spoke very little about my relationship with Melanie. Instead, we aimed our conversations toward my past: learning disabilities, my brothers, the anger I felt, and my violent fantasies. It soon became apparent that the breakup with Melanie, and even the breakup with Angela, were separate tips of a very large iceberg just below the surface of my disciplined, controlled life.

I sank deeper into the muddy ooze that filled the bottom of the dark well into which I had fallen. I struggled and grabbed for the slimy bank, attempting to pull myself to the wall and climb out. Each time I gripped the edge of the bank, I failed to get hold of it and slid back into the mire that now was up to my chin. Exhausted, I abandoned my attempts to reach the wall. My nose was barely above the filthy water line. So that was what it felt like to die?

I had been counseling with Betty Schull for about three months, and my depression remained as severe as the day I had begun. It was like being trapped in that pitch-black well, slowly sinking to the bottom. We were getting close to the core of the problem, and the poison was being forced to the surface, taking tremendous amounts of emotional energy with it. I didn't know how much more I was willing to take. Was it worth it? Couldn't I go back to living in my controlled world, the way I had before? No, it was too late. We had to get to the bottom of my severe depression, and the sooner the better.

> THE POISON WAS BEING FORCED TO THE SURFACE, TAKING TREMENDOUS AMOUNTS OF EMOTIONAL ENERGY WITH IT.

So I began to pull my head from the mud. I again

reached for the bank to drag myself ashore and start climbing out of the pit. From above me came a flicker of light. Looking up, I saw three figures standing at the lip of the well. They were very far away, mere dots peering down at me. Then I saw it—it was dangling from their hands, slowly coming toward me: a rope. I could make out the figures: Mark Rutledge was holding the coil of line, lowering it to me, while Terry Gillespie and Betty Schull looked on, encouraging me to tie the rope around my waist. Although they couldn't haul me up by themselves, they said they would do all they could to help me climb out. Gratefully, I seized the line and tied it about me. It was going to be a long climb.

That particular afternoon I was at one of my lowest points. The hot spring air drifting in through my window annoyed me. My blasting stereo couldn't dull the throb that ran through my skull. Looking at my calendar, I counted the days: three more until I was to see Betty Schull again. Maybe we'd make some sense of it all then. Had I really been seeing her for three months now? Listlessly, I fumbled with the pencil on my desk. How could I be so tired when I hadn't done a lick of work all day? I hated waking up from eight hours of sleep feeling as worn out as when I had fallen into bed.

A knock at the door startled me into movement. Shouting above the beat of my stereo, I called, "Come in."

Mark burst through the door. "How could you hear me knocking with all that music blasting?" he commented. "I don't see how you keep from going deaf."

Turning down the volume, I offered him a seat. It didn't take long for him to see that I was in another one of my depressive moods. "You want to talk about it, Evans?" he began in a more serious voice. He seemed to be ready to listen all night, if need be. I had never known a man like him before. He stopped in every day to check on me. He could hear what I said, remember it, and find a way to make me talk even in the most depressed mood. I didn't need to put on any airs with him; he accepted me as a friend no matter how far down I was. I didn't make much sense as I talked about keeping up the fight until I got to the core of my problem. But I was so tired, I wasn't sure if I was going to be able to keep up the pace. "Evans, buddy, you've got to stop being negative," Mark told me. "You're too hard on yourself. Ease off." Mark was incredibly affirming, always concentrating on my positive points, trying to build up my tattered confidence. We must have sat and talked for over two hours that breezy spring afternoon.

I couldn't believe what had happened to me. Here was Jamie Evans, a guy who only three months ago was a campus fellowship leader and minister, in desperate need himself of ministry. I realized now that God was forcing me to confront my own need for others. Suddenly my hyperproductive schedule had been shattered, and I was discovering the value of a relationship. Why had I missed that before? Until my junior year in college I had been content to be independent, almost a loner. Now I was too tired to go on that way. In Mark I had found a source of support and communication the likes of which I had never experienced before. How strange that it had taken an emotional crisis to teach me the incredible strength that lay in close friendship! What a teacher pain was turning out to be.

It didn't take long for Betty Schull to begin making sense out of my problem. One brilliant spring afternoon as I sat in her office, she showed me a part of myself I had never guessed was there. But it had a lot to do with my behavior.

"Jamie, I want you to listen very carefully now," she

said. "I think we may have come to the source of much of the trouble you've been having." Excited and hopeful, I sat up, waiting for the revelation. At last we were getting somewhere!

A lawnmower whirred by the window as the grounds crew struggled to keep up with the growth that surrounded our school. As the noise of the husky engine faded, Betty Schull explained: "The first day you came in here, you took control of the situation. With your yellow legal pad, you were all organized. You dominated the situation as you attempted to tell me all about you, and I let you do it. I wanted to watch you to see just how far you would go to dictate the session's proceedings. I wanted to see how much control you would try to put on me."

Readjusting herself in the chair, she tucked a leg under her and went on: "You need to control circumstances, people, schedules. You're very good at it. Have you noticed that?"

Shaking my head, I responded, "No. I'm pretty disciplined, but I never saw myself as controlling people."

"Well, you do, Jamie. You don't love yourself very much. You must remember that your lack of love is the basis for much of the depression, the need for control, and even the breakups with Angela, Melanie, and others."

Leaning back into the green cushions of the couch, I felt humiliated, wiped out. How long had I lived that way, totally unaware?

Betty continued: "Your learning disability took a heavy toll on your self-esteem. That is to be expected. It's not your fault that your self-esteem is low, so don't blame Jamie Evans for it. But Jamie Evans is responsible for working his way out of that situation. The rejection by your peers because of your hyperactivity, the poor grades and failures at school, the clumsiness and stuttering—all those things contributed to your thinking of yourself as bad, stupid, dumb. Subconsciously you thought you were bad, worthy of rejection.

"Then you were diagnosed and began a disciplined process of education. It brought you some affirmation, some successes in school, and some good relationships. Now there were two goals in your mind. Stealing mirrored the bad self-image you had: since you thought you were bad, you were going to act bad. But as your education and tutors helped you out of the academic problems of your LD, you were able to mask many of the negative feelings about yourself.

"I see your dyslexia as a two-front problem: number one is the academic side, which you have defeated. The fact that you're almost finished here at Wooster proves that. Number two is yet to be dealt with. That's the psychological side of dyslexia, the low self-image and lack of self-love. These I have confidence you will win over just as you did the academic side." She paused to answer the phone, annoyed that it had interrupted.

I picked up the small African jewelry box that was on the table separating us. I turned over its carved sides as I tried to organize all the information I had just received. I didn't want to lose even a particle of it.

Ending her phone conversation, Betty Schull apologized for the interruption and resumed her crossed-leg position.

"Dr. Schull, what caused me to dump Melanie and Angela the way I did?"

"I'm getting to that. Jamie, as you became more disciplined in school and your successes grew, the fear of academic failure faded, but the fear of being rejected remained. You found that if you could control people, you could avoid being rejected. By dominating conversations and being a leader, you found it easier to be accepted. But years later along came relationships that were more than superficial dating. I believe that with Angela and

Melanie you ran into a problem. The intimacies of a dating relationship are hard if not impossible to control. No
really vulnerable relationship can ever be dominated and
controlled for long. It takes too much energy on the con-
troller's part and suffocates the other person. Your low
self-opinion drove you to think you were going to be
rejected. After all, if you didn't love yourself, how could
you trust anyone else who claimed to love you?

"Isn't there a Bible verse about loving others as you
love yourself?" she asked, knowing very well there was
but testing me to find out if I was following her. "What
does that verse presuppose, Jamie?" Not waiting for me
to answer, she dove back in: "It presupposes the necessity
of self-love, self-trust, and self-acceptance before you can
give it to others, let alone receive it.

"You worked so hard to control your relationships with
the women you dated that you tired yourself out. As the
intimacy intensified and you got to know each other better, the control had to intensify accordingly. Vulnerability
frightened you terribly. What if she were to find out what
a dummy you really were? What if she saw what a bad
person she was dating? She'd dump you outright. That's
what your mind kept telling you, so you never let anyone
get close. Jamie, it's very difficult to control someone and
to always dominate the conversation. It tires one out and
kills the joy that dating can be. You ran from those
women because you were tired of having to control the
situation, and that reduced your delight in the relationship."

Looking at me, she smiled. "You've won half the battle
already. You know what you have to work on now, and
you're willing to seek the help you need to win. This
week I want you to think, consciously, that you are good.
I want you to avoid dominating conversations and situations. Relax; trust other people and yourself enough to
let go of the hypercontrol. You'll be amazed at the way
creativity grows when there are two people participating

in a relationship, as opposed to one person pulling all the strings."

Leaving the student health center, I walked by the geology building on my way back to my room. Its old brick exterior gave it a well-used appearance. I was excited for the first time in months. I could hardly wait to get back to my room and write down what we had unearthed that day. I was not about to forget what I was paying such a high price in emotional pain to learn.

A strange feeling swept through me. For a moment I didn't want the pain to go away. It was driving me to get help, to see parts of myself I had never dreamed existed. Through the pain God was driving me to grow as I never had grown before. My Christian faith had never been so rich as when, crying, I would be forced to kneel before my God and beg for the strength to make it through one more day. The Lord always answered with just enough energy to last me until the next night, when again I'd be forced to come to him. At those times when the depression had been especially destructive, he had sent my friends Mark and Terry to help me carry the load. The timing of their visits was too exact to be coincidence; they had been sent!

It had been a year since I began my counseling. Slowly, as the Wooster winter dragged on, I felt my confidence building. Not the old confidence rooted in secure schedules and control, but a certainty that in myself I was a worthy person. I no longer needed to be the super-disciplined fanatic. To be sure, there had been a place for that in my earlier life. If I had not developed good work and control habits as a child, I would not have been as successful in defeating learning disability. But those days were gone. Although I would always have a trace of stuttering, be hyperactive to a mild degree, and read slowly, I had learned to compensate for my disorder. School was no longer a battlefield but a pleasure.

Now my habits had to change. The first battle had been won; it was time to move to the next. Relationships, self-esteem, vulnerability—they were the goals set before me. For a time during my counseling I had been reluctant to take them on. Hadn't one disability been enough? Did I have to start a whole new fight? I found my answer in the book of Hebrews.

In Hebrews 12 we are told that being a Christian doesn't mean an easy life. And in my case, my difficulties brought me closer to God. In that sense they were a blessing and were to be, yes, relished. I began to learn what Christ meant by saying we must love him above even our own families or lives. Laughing inwardly, I remembered a friend who claimed that Christianity was a crutch. It had hardly been one in my experience. I had lived through a time when God demanded that I walk through my own personal hell, literally a valley of the shadow of death. There had been moments when death had smelled sweet compared to the pain of struggling on with the continual depression and anxiety of those early counseling days. It had seemed easier to say no to life, to withdraw into passivity and sink into depression's jaws. But God had demanded a resounding yes to life. He had demanded faith even where there seemed to be so little. And faith had responded. Faith had grown.

Now it was time to confront the anger from all those early years. If I could deal with it once and for all by going home and encountering the source, I would be free.

Starting up my blue Toyota one spring morning I drove out of Wooster toward D.C., an eight-hour journey I knew well. My mind was locked on one thing: clear the decks of all unneeded baggage. This anger was certainly unneeded. I was nervous during that drive. How would my family respond? They knew I was coming, and I had written to my oldest brother and my father explaining my intent. They both had welcomed the opportunity. I was expected.

Dan was five years my senior. We sat down in the stuffed blue chairs in the living room. My parents weren't home yet, and Dan had just returned from the congressional office where he worked. Kicking off his loafers, he prepared to talk, his khaki trousers and oxford shirt marking him as a "preppy." It didn't seem so long ago that I knew him as the La Jolla surfer trooping off to the beach and never taking me along.

> MY MIND WAS LOCKED ON ONE THING: CLEAR THE DECKS OF ALL UNNEEDED BAGGAGE. THIS ANGER WAS CERTAINLY UNNEEDED.

"Was I such a terrible little brother, such an obnoxious brat?" I began. "Aren't big brothers supposed to look out for the kids in the family? Why didn't we once do something together?"

"Jamie, your hyperactivity made you tough to be with, but that wasn't the whole reason for our avoidance of you," Dan explained. "We were really caught up in the beach scene those days. It was cool to do your own thing, not the family thing. They were strange times, the sixties. Families weren't the center of life, and especially not little brothers. Tim and I really ribbed you then, and we both feel bad about it now. I apologize."

I knew he meant it.

"Also, Jamie," Dan continued, "we Evans men are pretty independent people and we don't like being dominated. There were times when you were almost overwhelming."

I knew what he was driving at. My control techniques had worked well with people outside the family, who were more willing to let me take the lead, but my father and brothers were leaders in their own right and weren't about to be dominated by a younger family member. I could remember a number of occasions when my brothers' wills and mine had clashed and ended up in bloodied noses. In order to compensate for my fear of rejection, I had tried to take control, only to be rebuked and—as I interpreted it in those painful days—rejected in my own family. No wonder I spent so much time away from home! No wonder I had lived so independently at school, or traveling, or anywhere.

"It seems I owe you an apology, too, Dan," I said. "I'll do my best to ease up on the control, especially with you, Tim, and Dad."

MY VISIT HOME AND THE HONESTY I WAS ABLE TO SHARE WITH MY FAMILY DID MUCH TO EASE THE TENSION INSIDE ME.

Dan and I began spending a great deal of time together, especially when I stayed at my folks' home on Capitol Hill, which was just across the street from Dan's apartment in the big old house he and his partners bought, restored, and managed. Dan and I began building a strong friendship, and I found the brotherhood I missed in La Jolla. Our mutual apologies were more an affirmation of our present closeness than forgiveness for past faults. I know now that Dan is a spiritual brother as well as a blood brother, and a confidant I will have for life.

Although my sister, Andie, and I had very little direct

contact until then, she too felt a need to talk during my visit home. The morning after Dan and I talked, I went to the apartment where Andie lived with her husband, Craig. Immediately I was struck by the smell of a good breakfast cooking.

Sitting at the kitchen table along with Andie, Dan, and Craig, we plunged into food and conversation. Andie has a way of being so direct and honest that it didn't take us long to get to the heart of the matter. She and I talked about the reasons for our distance during the early years of my life and about our growing desire for closeness and communication. It was very much like my conversation with Dan the night before. Both Andie and I were now able to see each other as the kind of persons who meant something to each other. We both apologized for past misunderstandings and hurts.

Then Craig, in his perceptive, quiet manner, said, "Jamie, this is good." With a nod of approval and satisfaction, he put his blessing on our time together. As a newcomer to the family, Craig has a clarity of understanding that I relish. I appreciate his comments and his friendship, and the way he helps all of us to see ourselves from a refreshing point of view.

My visit home and the honesty I was able to share with my family did much to ease the tension inside me. Tim was in New York and therefore I'd have to wait to get things straight with him. But I would do it. I knew it was important, even though it might be painful. I was learning how essential it was to be able to see my family as an emotional resource during my time of counseling and self-examination. And for the first time I could remember, I actually longed to be home, basking in the warmth I knew was there, allowing it to strengthen me for the next phase of my battle against disability.

On my way back to school to prepare for exams, I felt a new freedom inside me. The anger was gone, and in

its place I had the love and support of my whole family.
I soaked up every bit of it.

Tossing my running shoes into the small dorm closet next
to the door of my room, I changed into walking shoes
as Mark fiddled with my stereo tuner. We were planning
to see *Chariots of Fire* with a gang from our fellowship.
A knock at the door brought me from the closet still
tying my shoe, and when I opened the door I almost fell
over from surprise. It was my other brother Tim, four
years older, who had driven all the way from upper New
York State where he was working on a grant to get his
Ph.D. in medical research. Tim and I had rarely seen
each other during my college career. Now he was standing before me, suitcase in hand.

"Hey, Jamie," he said, "thought I might come down
and see you on your turf for a few days."

"Er . . . great, Tim, I didn't know you were coming
down, but you're more than welcome. Come on in, this
is Mark Rutledge." Shaking hands with my brother, Mark
made a hasty retreat from the room. He knew how little
I had seen Tim during the past few years and figured
that his presence would be more appreciated elsewhere.
As Mark left, I felt strangely anxious. I was a blood
brother to the man standing before me, yet I hardly knew
him.

How was I going to keep a conversation going for a
few days with a guy I hardly knew? As usual, I was taking
responsibility for the success or failure of the visit, which
I had neither expected nor initiated. But Tim wasn't
about to be controlled.

"I thought I'd stop by and relax for a few days during
my break," he said. "I've brought my books and notes
and thought maybe we could study here together." Al-

ready he was defusing much of the tension by letting me know that I wouldn't have to entertain him while he was there. "We'll study, and when we're ready to talk, we'll talk," he continued.

And that is precisely what we did. During the three days Tim stayed at Wooster, I slowly began to know a very special man. My blue-eyed, blond-haired, six-foot-three brother is a quiet person gifted with a brilliant mind for science. He plays classical guitar and loves a good Russian novel. In short, he is quite the opposite of me. In my cluttered room we talked late into the evenings— about family, about the past, and about the future. It was Tim's way of making up for the years of silence. Although there were no outright apologies from either of us, as there had been between Dan and me, a subtle peace settled over me. Tim wouldn't have come if he hadn't cared. The fact he did that was enough to end the anger I had harbored toward him for so long.

CHAPTER 13

Working Stiff

Fourteen years have passed since I finished chapter twelve. I am married now and a father of two beautiful children. We no longer live in the East but are situated among the pines and rocky shores of the central coast of California where I am a pastor of a Presbyterian church. Circumstantially, much has changed about my life, yet I remain within quite the same person. As an adult I have watched my learning difference take on new and subtle shades. On occasion it fades into the near haze of the past, yet it also has the power to resurrect old habits amid new challenges.

Hope abounds for my kind in this new era of education. Much research and remediation is now available for the learning-differenced community that was not available during my educational years. Public and private schools alike have adopted testing and training practices that identify and serve children at the earliest stages of struggle with their LD issues. Whether the categories are Attention-Deficit/Hyperactivity Disorder in some states or Perceptually Impaired in other states, all school systems are light years ahead of the dismal past, when even the existence of such differences was doubted.

Yet as an adult I find little research or remediation available for the more mature of the LD community. This field of the adult ramifications of dyslexia is still a virgin track. In this chapter we will explore a few of those new frontiers in hopes of stimulating conversation and analysis of what the adult LD wrestles with.

After thirty-eight years of life within my body you would think I would know my own idiosyncrasies. Yet on that cold winter's day, cold for California's coast, I found myself perplexed. It was nearing one-thirty in the afternoon, and I was writing a sermon for the following Sunday. My secretary knocked on my office door and entered to ask me a question concerning our order of service for that week. I noticed a flash of emotion deep within. *How dare she interrupt me during this time of study! Can't I get any peace and quiet?* My short temper nearly rose to the surface, but after years of such afternoon emotions I knew better than to show my actual feelings.

> **AFTER THIRTY-EIGHT YEARS OF LIFE WITHIN MY BODY YOU WOULD THINK I WOULD KNOW MY OWN IDIOSYNCRASIES.**

"Yes, Fran, that ordering sounds excellent and please include the baptism segment for the eighth as well. Be sure to check spelling on the hymn, too, as the computer stumbles on the old words." This I said through a plastic smile that hid the boil of peevish emotion just centimeters beneath the surface. Once she departed I quietly stood, closed the door, and retook my seat. As I picked up my pencil and retrained my attention toward the sermon, I saw my hand trembling. At the same time my mind flitted to the window and attention flagged. I had to drag it back to the task, but my shaking hand continued. A slow yet annoying buzz began between my ears signaling the onset of my afternoon's high—buzzing energy surging through the mind, raving emotions that have little connection with real circumstances, and a constant need to do self-checks to remain sociable even while wanting to scream and run away into the hills to be alone. Concentration lags as energy gets used up in the effort to pay attention.

On this particular day I had done what I could to postpone this "high." I had run five miles that morning before coming into the office. My breakfast and lunch had been long on the carbohydrates and short on the processed sugars. I had gotten good rest, for at last the baby was sleeping through the night. But even with all of these fixes in place, I still had to deal with the inevitable remnants of growing up with hyperactivity. I had not grown out of this aspect of my LD. I had simply learned how to delay, and to a degree control, its wild careening drive through my day.

It is a muggy and dark September day. The leaves are fluttering nervously, while the air is pregnant with the threat of rain, and there's enough humidity in the soaked air to make us all sweat at the first sign of movement.

You'd think in all this dreary weather that I would want to settle into a book and a comfortable chair and relax. You would be dead wrong. I have been a beast today to friend and foe. My poor wife has had to put up with my moods, which have been largely akin to the temper of a restless gorilla caged up during mating season. Sitting is the last thing that I want to do. I am easily irritated, slow of mind and sharp of tongue. What troubles me? Too little exercise over the past two days. I'm "hyper." After a six-mile run or a solid workout, I'll be a new man. My mind will be back on line, my emotions will be settled, while my patience factor will be up by the power of ten.

I have lived so long in this state that you'd think that I would have gotten a handle on this, but too often I forget to do what I must to control the sine curve of energy that I live with. You see, my energy is built in erratic pulses, much like the sine curves we supposedly studied in high school. A sine curve is a wide series of valleys and mountains with very little flat space or plains in between. Either I'm up or down, not much on a flat level. If you met me, you would probably not notice me climbing ceilings or crawling the walls. That's because through great desire and discipline I've fooled you. I use my body chemicals to help myself. My chemical of choice is the body's own endorphines, opiate-like substances secreted when we exercise hard. They bring a sense of euphoria in the short term, and in the long term they produce a clarity and ability to control concentration, speech, and my ever-moving limbs. (For me "long-term" is about three hours on a good day.)

Science also offers hyperactive people Ritalin and other drugs that seem to release chemicals in our brains that allow us to block out distractions and slow down enough to adapt to a culture that sits. I personally never favored taking medication, and about 20 percent of the male ADHD population don't tolerate Ritalin well. But others find it very helpful, virtually essential.

When I'm up on my sine curve, when the energy is bursting out at the proverbial seams, I am a sponge for information, I talk too fast, and I slur too much. I am on the loud side, and my behavior is big, full of exaggerated emotions and wide swings of topic in conversation.

I act in ways that are not appropriate and stumble into and then out of trains of thought, leaving others breathless from trying to keep up. I am easily distracted in these moments, but that is also true of my lows on the sine curve. Some things are consistent at least. But there is a definite wonder to these highs: nature sparkles to life and beauty is easily seen, ideas flare with energetic fire, and in athletics the high makes me able to run and jump and play with boundless zest. Movement, especially that of animals, is easily picked out. It's as if my focus is wide-angle and my sensitivity to all around me is magnified. Social nuances become clear as others are observed reacting to people and events around them. Unfortunately, I tend to be blind to how I affect people during my highs. It is a wonder and a drag. Life seems new and boundless even as there is a loneliness because so few people can sense it with us.

The lows on this human sine curve are dull, listless, and moody. Perception is slow, speech is forced, and the desire to withdraw is strong. Anxiety appears frequently in this state, and motivation tends to be low. Negative thoughts abound, and I itch to pick a fight—anything to bounce me out of the listlessness. I know many of my kind were first to volunteer for the Crusades or to sail with Columbus just to find some diversion for these lows. My kind were born to move and roam, not sit.

> **I CAN BEST DESCRIBE THESE SURGES IN ENERGY AS AKIN TO THE FEELING OF AN ALL-NIGHTER WITH FAR TOO MUCH COFFEE.**

I have this nightmare: I awake in the glare of fluorescent lights with the smell of strong disinfectant in my nose and a burning in my neck. I close my eyes, hoping to remember what it was that I was doing that brought me to this place. I recall the squeal of brakes, sheet metal tearing, and the flash of my body slamming into a hard, unyielding object, then nothing. It becomes clearer now. Car accident. My little coupe met something bigger and lost in the collision. I'm in a hospital, there is a steel halo around my head, and nothing below my neck moves. I've broken my spinal cord and I am paralyzed. It dawns on me that though my body is now permanently inactive, my hyperactivity rages. Now there is no release to be found in exercise. I will suffer the surges of highs and lows with no endorphines, no peace. We all have our deepest dreads. This is mine—to be captive to my energy, not its master. I strive to care for my muscles and joints, especially my knees, for these are my therapy, my sweet release. My knees through running give me control.

I can best describe these surges in energy as akin to the feeling of an all-nighter of study with far too much coffee in your system and way too little sleep. It's a feeling of hollow energy that buzzes and wriggles through you, yet in its lows it bequeathes no real strength to the body. The highs are best described as if someone had decelerated the rest of the population. I am the only one moving at a normal speed. Others' pace is maddeningly slow, especially in conversation, and I find myself ending their sentences for them just to hurry them along.

When I met David, he was a missionary for a foreign translating ministry. David was in his early forties, and only two years ago had been diagnosed as having Attention-Deficit/Hyperactivity Disorder. His story was consistent with those who are told later in life that they are not dumb or undisciplined, but clearly wired differently than the rest of the population. He was struggling to find ways to adjust his energy, direct his focus, and smooth his rough relationships. David was tall but had the far too lean, almost cavernous look of one who consumes calories by the triple digits simply by walking down the hall. He was a furnace of energy.

He had been placed on Dexedrin by his psychiatrist. It, a medicine like Ritalin, had worked wonders to moderate the highs and lows. He was socially more adept and his relationship with his wife was improving, yet he still knew that he wanted to be in control and capable without the drug. On too many occasions he had forgotten to take his medicine and had found himself back in his old patterns of behavior. Sticking to a task was almost impossible, both in his daily routine and in his broader plans, for he found himself easily distracted and bored. Movement seemed his only elixir. On one such occasion he was brought up short by one of his coworkers. Apparently David, in trying to make his point on some ministry option, had emotionally run over his audience with overstatement and zeal.

Drug therapy, whether it be from exercise or from a pharmacy, can and does work to prevent further esteem loss and social blunders while to a moderate degree raising esteem. But drug therapy does not encourage us to develop the essential tools within ourselves for control. Somewhere we must find the key to unlock our own resources of confidence and understanding. David now knew, thanks to drug treatment, how good it could feel to be more normal and socially adept. Yet he had no permanent hold on how to remain in this state without medication.

I wish there were an option beyond such dependence and sustained therapy. Part of me is deeply grateful for those little Ritalin pills. They offer me some form of release on a long-term basis, but I also loathe the thought of having to resort to them should my body no longer be capable of serious exercise. I pray to God that researchers will find another way, and soon!

I believe in reality. I want desperately to live in a reality that accepts situations as they are and not as I want them to be. Since the world's population cannot be expected to keep pace with my fluctuating energy curves, it is obvious that I must be the one to adjust to their more even patterns. I have come to accept that *personality modification* will probably always have to be a tool in my relational repertoire. But that's the case for all of us, isn't it? All of us grow up with at least a few traits that rub others the wrong way or get us into hot water—a quick temper, an inability to keep track of details, a problem being on time. Most people spend a good part of their lives compensating for such weaknesses *while* trying to accept themselves in spite of their weaknesses.

I have had to learn to mistrust my first inclinations and impulses. I must start with a dedication to focusing. Though my first impulse is to follow movement, say the squirrel that just darted across the lawn beyond my office window, I force myself to stay present with the man in the chair across from me who is seeking counsel about his marriage. This focusing can be a denial of all the strengths of observation that I have, while it is an elevation of concentration, one of my least gifted areas. But my job demands such concentration if I am to really hear the pains and struggles of the people I yearn to minister to in my congregation.

Control is the cousin of focusing. This control takes energy. Sitting attentively consumes vast resources of my energy, while walking or running seems to energize me. This is the upside-down world of the ADHD individual.

Sitting still and listening is torture, but give me miles of open road to explore or ocean to swim, and I am in heaven. There are no shortcuts to such focus. I find prayer especially daunting, for being open, listening, and passive to the dominant Spirit of God makes prayer at its best contrary to my core instincts of activism and mental busyness. But focus I must if I am ever to be still and know my God.

Thus it occurs to me that some parts of who I am must be retrained if I am to be both a pastor and a seeker of God. One hour of prayer and passivity, stillness and listening, earns me one hour of crashing rock music and a long run. An afternoon of sitting and counseling wins me a session with my beloved old two-liter engine, hands busy, with no one else to focus on. Please understand: I adore prayer and truly care for the people God has called me to minister to in this marvelous community. I would be desperately lonely and shallow without both, but the cost is heavy.

> I BELIEVE IN REALITY. I WANT DESPERATELY TO LIVE IN A REALITY THAT ACCEPTS SITUATIONS AS THEY ARE AND NOT AS I WANT THEM TO BE.

I find this is especially critical in terms of emotions. When the highs and lows of the energy curve bring extreme waves of mood, often I must say bluntly and even ruthlessly, "Emotions, you lie! Be gone! Are my feelings in line?" If not, then I must adjust. I am confident that as the years pass my self-reorienting will become less and less necessary, for I will learn the appropriate emotional response and adapt. If I could conquer the word and letter reversals of my early dyslexia, consciously unreversing then what now is natural and automatic, then my emotions can also be so trained. The outward observer may find this process of emotional checking rather comical. I lag behind some others in my emotional reactions, since most folk react instantly. (And get themselves in trouble for it!) Yet optimism is on my side, for the time is getting shorter and shorter between each action and its appropriate emotional response. I am learning, and with God's help will soon be able, to react evenly and calmly most of the time.

CHAPTER 14

Romance Is in the Air

My first memories of her were from thirty years ago in La Jolla, California, during the mid-1960s. She was six years my junior, had blue eyes and blond hair, and was even then tall and freckled. Our fathers had served together in two churches, so the Hess family was as close to us as nonfamily can be. Kristy was part of my world from the start of my memories. But my family's move to the East Coast put a temporary gulf between us.

Twenty years later she arrived in my city of Washington, D.C., and worked for my brother in a congressional office. She had grown into a tall and attractive young woman. It was a no-brainer to fall for her as I did.

Our courtship was anything but normal, though. *Intense:* That is the word that most clearly describes the degree of this courtship. As with all else in me, there was little balance to my pursuit of my future wife. I courted her recklessly and impetuously. I thank my God that Kristy Hess was a known quantity to my family, of strong character and deep faith. Otherwise my clan would have had good reason for real concern. I was not known to be a wise judge of character, and in matters romantic this could be dangerous. I leapt way too fast and with little forethought. Perhaps I could rephrase a cliché: "Only fools and the hyperactive rush in." Of course, most young men feel this way, yet I am certain that my hyperactivity increased it.

I am learning that character analysis requires observation and time to muse. One must stop one's own movement long enough to view those around and learn what marks the character within. An old friend of mine always used golf to instruct him in the inner worlds of his pals. He would watch for impatience on the course, how the ball was approached, how the player took a bad score or the need to wait for a slower group. Would the golfer allow another to play through, and how did he deal with those playing better or worse than himself? I have missed much in the study of humanity by my sheer speed of action and my lack of the kind of quiet and intent observation that my friend uses on the golf course.

Much observation goes into choosing one's life partner. One looks for a moral and spiritual dimension of compatibility, plus a mutuality of intelligence and emotional depth. Interests and passions, political views and habits, play and fun, all these are forced to mesh in a dynamic interplay. It takes time to discover these in one another and to discern true compatibility. The choice must be wise, prayerful, and patiently pursued. In my relationship with Kristy, that patience would prove to be more than just a little difficult. There is a pacing in conversation that must be observed: not too deep too fast. Don't reveal your whole self and your secrets until trust is established. Time together, too, has a gradual and building progression as well as expressions of growing affection. Yet the hyperactive part of me extends beyond the mechanical. It is not just sitting still that causes frustration but also emotional and romantic pacing. I want to move, now!

During our early dates I was not the only suitor pursuing Kristy. This in itself was a gift from on high, for to a degree it regulated our intensity. She saw to it that time was shared and that the pace was seemly and healthy. She would not be pushed or railroaded. She had a strength and character that resisted unhealthy demands.

In D.C. summer evenings could be magical times. The heat of the swamp in which we lived lifted to a degree, a cooler river breeze clearing the fetid humidity slightly. The town would come alive with couples. Union Station was our favorite haunt as we courted. Theaters, food courts, stores, and cafés lined the wonderfully remodeled old structure, once condemned for its general dilapidation. These were D.C.'s best years during the early 1990s. There was a sense that the city might be moving beyond its

> ONLY FOOLS
> AND THE
> HYPERACTIVE
> RUSH IN.

chronic decay. As we left our movie, a science fiction thriller (I knew she must love me when she consented to go to such films with me), we wandered out to the parking lot and climbed into my old Honda. With the windows open and the stereo playing romantic rock, I drove us down Massachusetts Avenue. Despite the city's problems, it does have the nation's best architectural diversity. "Mass Ave" is a showcase for homes and embassies in the best of many architectural styles. Mile after mile of well-pruned trees and manicured hedges frame glorious works of domestic art.

"So what's your favorite?" I asked. She pointed left down a side street and we glided to a stop before a Tudor-styled embassy.

"I like this best at night," she admitted. "I can peek into the lit living rooms and see how they are decorated and what the feeling of the house is all about. Look there." Just then a well-dressed couple opened their front door and greeted guests just exiting a limousine with a nation's flag that I did not recognize flying from it. The entry hall was festooned with tapestries, an armored knight, and a liveried servant bearing a tray of drinks—nation states going about their international relations work with flair on a warm summer's evening.

Next to the mansion stood a gatekeeper's cottage. "Now that is my kind of home," I said and went on to explain. "See the gables and the steep roof line? The rooms in there would be perfect for a kid, and the yard is excellent for a dog or two. There is a place to raise a family. Even the den is set up with a rolltop desk for my study and we . . ." I stopped long enough in my reverie to look at Kristy's widening eyes. We had been dating for a few months, but not exclusively, and she had made no mention of any desire to spend the rest of her life with me. Here I was house shopping and planning for domestic life. Her wide eyes said it all. I realized my blunder. "Getting just a tad ahead of ourself aren't we, lad?" I teasingly chided myself out loud, hoping to make the moment more humorous than inappropriate. She shook her head and smirked. I think she had me figured out long before this occasion of feasting on my own foot.

Fortunately for me, Kristy trusted the Evans clan as much as we trusted the Hess family. I, too, was a known quantity. It would seem she was disposed to trusting me despite my overeager approach.

As a pastor I am eager to see those marriages that I perform last a lifetime. As a person with a learning difference, I know that many of us with learning disabilities run the risk of divorce. In fact, statistically the numbers are clear—we are high-risk spouses for divorce. When pastors begin the process of counseling a couple prior to marriage, we are trained to look for red flags—areas of potential relational danger and unseen baggage that might explode later to wreak havoc on family life.

The impatience and impetuosity of the hyperactive person as well as the underdeveloped ability to observe social consequences makes for a bull in a marital china shop. We know there is trouble, we see the broken plates and saucers, yet we are at a loss to understand how our deeds in any way brought this to be. And doubling the trouble, we may have yet to learn how to really hear the cries of frustration from those we love. If this is hard for those who are diagnosed and consciously struggling with their learning difference, you can imagine how hard this is for the undiagnosed. Unaware, they blunder into relational disease, insensitively running over those whom they love the most, ignorant of the obvious consequences.

My advice to myself on this score is to remember to be aware of how I make others feel and react. If I am unaware of my poor social interaction, I can at least key into the responses of others. Are they frustrated? Do they exit a conversation abruptly? What do their facial expressions communicate? Are they eager to be in my company? Do they look at me when they talk to me?

It is both a truism and a struggle that I feel most normal when I am operating about 40 percent

I FEEL MOST NORMAL WHEN I AM OPERATING ABOUT 40 PERCENT FASTER THAN FOLK AROUND ME.

faster than folk around me. In this comfort zone I will jump from topic to topic as my mind makes connections that to many are not logical but rather wildly tangential!

One of my dear friends and mountain biking adventurers knows this well. He recently confided in me, "Jamie, I was hurt at first when you would dart from topic to topic in the early days of our friendship." His name is Kin Lancaster, and he cares enough about our friendship to tell me the truth. We were riding up a coastal peak at the time, and I was too exhausted to retort.

Kin continued, "But then I got to know you and realized that your mind does that automatically, that it wasn't an insult, and that it didn't mean you weren't interested in what I had to say. I also got used to repeating my life's details because you would frequently forget them."

We rode up the creek trail in silence for a moment. I was agonized by the degree of climb and our rate of pedaling, but I wanted to figure this out with him before we began our descent. He rides like a Baptist fleeing bars when we go downhill, and I would have no chance to catch him once that wild ride began. It occurred to me that under normal, rested circumstances I would avoid such hopping and tangential conversation because I would be consciously editing my comments to conform with expected social standards. I call this *self-editing*. It takes concentration and energy but allows me to master a high level of social discourse.

What had gone wrong with Kin? With him I had fallen back into social habits that I had thought I had beaten years ago. By this time my legs began to spasm and the ride took on a new degree of pain. Sweat dripped down my nose and tickled my upper, unshaven lip, finally settling on the precipice some people call my chin. It began to make sense. Most of my time with Kin was spent in excruciating, thrilling, and awesome athletics along the most beautiful coastlines of California. My mind was too distracted and too tired to do the normal work of social adjustment. Add to this the fact that I felt able to be myself with this friend, and you have the makings of my relational style. I simply was being myself.

One of the beauties of courtship with Kristy was the acceptance that even the hyper Jamie, when he would make his abrupt and uninvited appearance, was loved and found endearing. It is deeply reassuring to have been discovered for who one really is and to be appreciated all the same.

Early on in our courtship Kristy knew when I was tired or deeply distracted, for I would allow the fast-talking Jamie to surface. That Jamie tried to be witty but ended up being ridiculous. He made silly rhymes and jingles, talked at 240 words a minute, stuttered, leapt from theme to theme, and exaggerated profusely and without regard to the truth—as long as it sounded good—and used large hand gestures. His mood swung, and he mentally focused or obsessed on singular themes.

Perhaps this mental obsessing put the most strain on our dating life. We now call this monomania. Some call it obsessive-compulsive behavior or hyperfocus. In any case, it is clearly a kind of focus that blocks out all else until the issue is resolved.

Every couple wrestles with issues that require conversation and compromise. With me the wrestling is almost Herculean. I want to fix it and fix it now, even if that means talking until two in the morning. Problematic projects present the same hurdle for me. It is not uncommon to find me in the garage until all hours of the night attempting to fix a car that refuses to cooperate. I forget to eat, sleep, or communicate with others. My focus excludes all else. I feel anxious if I choose to leave the task or topic undone.

Kristy and I have learned to laugh at this little monster of obsessiveness. We now have a rule that after ten in the evening no deep or difficult talks are allowed. I am learning the wisdom of letting an issue sit and percolate for a spell, revisiting it as new understandings arise and having the confidence and patience to know that time is a friend. Conclusion without insight is no conclusion at all. Even my projects are slowly being spaced out, done in increments. If the engine is not fully rebuilt by tonight, it certainly won't know the difference. But find me tired or stressed, and I quickly abandon these newfound habits.

I am not entirely sure of the source of this monomania, but I have noted it in other adults. We forget pacing and balance. We allow ourselves to become overwhelmed and are anxiously restless until a matter is resolved. Part of the source may be a lack of confidence that we have the innate skills to work out our problems gently, patiently, and naturally. We must take control and do it now lest we face failure later. Or perhaps it stems from a consuming view of the present—"now" is so real and so emotionally charged that "later" has little value or reality. We are impetuous therefore because waiting is agonizing. We don't put matters on the back burner well. It's as if we are a single-burner stove in a world that asks for some pots to simmer while the cooking goes on.

THE JOURNEY TO THE GOAL WAS AS IMPORTANT AS THE GOAL ITSELF.

Another reason for this may be an attempt to keep life both simple and stimulating. When I find a task that gives me satisfaction, I may neglect other priorities to continue on that pleasurable course. This falls into the category of being either "on" or "off" in my interests. I desire to learn the measured life of a more even interest level. As a practice in this regard I will intentionally leave a project in midstream, returning later refreshed and with renewed creativity. Still, the delay weighs on me. Why would I ever want to delay until tomorrow what I can quickly do today? I am learning that the answer to this siren song is the truth that many tasks, if done well, will take more time and energy than one day affords. Indeed, no great task can be quickly or thoughtlessly finished.

Dating Kristy reinforced this measured approach to life. This great task would surely not be finished quickly, nor should it, for in the courtship itself there was much pleasure and learning to be done above and beyond the aim of marriage. The journey to the goal was as important as the goal itself.

Courtship found me laughing more than I ever had before. Kristy's family, especially her younger brother Bradley, have a lot of fun. Until recently I found humor hard to get and harder still to accomplish. Now, after seven years of marriage, I am beginning at least to get it.

Mental quickness, a turn of phrase, keen social awareness, and confidence all seem essential to humor. But there is also a measure of surprise, the unexpected conclusion, and timing. When I laugh at Bradley's jokes or his keen impersonations, I forget myself, my self-editing, and my learning difference. There is such a marvelous release in humor. I watch him as he weaves a tale. He takes his time, notes the interest of his audience, plays them unawares, and then springs his ending, and inevitably we laugh until we hurt. You can't plan or control this kind of conversation. It comes from deep within, a wit and a confidence that says that I am not only worth listening to but able to create that pleasure in the audience that erupts into laughter. It's both powerful and joyous. I have met few really funny people with learning differences.

When Kristy would laugh after I told a story or when I would inadvertently crack a joke and her family would chuckle, I would pause and wonder. This was new. In-

evitably, I was relaxed, not rushed or controlled, and doing less editing than usual. Moments like these were rare
but growing glacially more frequent. This seemed tied to
the growth of intimacy and confidence in our courtship.
Something was happening in my core that was neither
expected nor planned. A natural confidence was welling
up from some unseen pool of grace.

This love brought inklings of a kind of life of security
and acceptance that I was unprepared for. I am sure that
Christ himself works through such holy unions as marriage to bring healing. In my past tutors were employed,
counselors engaged, and lessons taught by curriculum.
But here in courtship and then marriage there was a
process of learning and growing that I had not expected.
Its health benefits showed in my growing habit of laughter and even a bemused outlook on my own still slow
social ability. When I opened my eyes and really looked,
the world sparkled with mirth. I will not reduce this to
simple romanticism and giggling infatuation. This was
broader. I was waking up more and more not with a list
of to-do's in my businesslike head but with a sense of
well-being and even a chuckle or two. I was changing.
Was this what the rest of the world occasionally did?
The love of an emotionally healthy woman is a won-
drous thing.

This courtship also brought me to a direct collision
with the old forces of fear and control. In college I had
bailed out of a number of dating relationships due to a
lack of confidence and a fear of commitment. If one has
a low opinion of oneself, then intimacy brings on fear of
rejection. After all, who could love the real you? To avoid
being rejected, I rejected others first. Fear is a bad foundation for a dating relationship.

By the time I was thirty and beginning to pursue my
future wife, I was in a different world. The fear was largely
gone. Time had worked along with my deep satisfaction

in my employment. The job used a number of my skills in an environment that made success almost inevitable. I was a teacher and chaplain at a private school. The classroom was perfect for my energy and need to move around, while the academic load kept my mind growing and challenged. My students were the cream of the crop. They were eager, no more than eighteen per class, and well disciplined. I was encouraged to teach Russian and Soviet history, U.S. history, ethics, and to preach in the weekly chapel service. I lived on campus as a dormitory master

WHEN I OPENED MY EYES AND REALLY LOOKED, THE WORLD SPARKLED WITH MIRTH.

and thus my life was simple, focused, and well rewarded. The school was supportive of its faculty, the headmaster was a solid and capable Christian leader, while the grounds were aesthetically fabulous. I thrived! This was the same school that had deeply ministered to me as a student eight years prior. St. Albans afforded me time and space to grow into the confidence that is essential to intimate commitments.

Kristy and I spent our first three years of marriage there. Those were halcyon days for us, full of play and discovery. True, I had to learn how to be a husband, but the course work had its benefits, and marriage fit with my values and view of what adulthood should look like. Had I known in college how groundless my fears were, I would have learned how to laugh and love much earlier.

CHAPTER 15

Life's Seasons Move On

The last of the oil dripped from the reservoir and pooled in the plastic bucket that was stationed directly beneath. I inserted the plug, tightened it, and installed the oil filter, carefully securing it one-half turn after contact with its seal. Next came the fill of the crank case with four quarts of oil and the job was complete. I scanned the underside of the car. This was my territory, familiar, safe, and deeply comfortable. I knew the hoses, wires, and systems by task and past maintenance. Seeing no oil leaks, I wiped my hands and scanned the yard for Kristy, my new wife. I was eager to show her how I was caring for her car, no doubt hoping for a pat on the head for being such a capable husband. I loved this woman, and I was eager to demonstrate it.

Not seeing her on that glorious Washington, D.C., spring morning, I started to wash and wax, vacuum, and generally detail her automobile. It had been two hours since I had left our apartment, and still she did not come to inspect my work as she would occasionally do. I jogged upstairs and called for her. From our light-filled living room came her voice, followed by wafts of rich coffee aroma. I hate coffee.

"Still drinking that poison? Hey, I finished the car, do you want to come and inspect it?" I hopefully queried.

"No, thanks." I heard her say this but could not see her, for she was reading an article in a magazine and did not look up. Kristy's lack of enthusiasm triggered an alarm bell in the back of my mind, warning me to wake up. I move fast and often think later, but I was learning to look for cues in relationships that alerted me to what was happening beneath the surface. I sensed that something wasn't right and stopped my mouth and feet long enough to take a reading.

Little did I know that I was about to stumble upon one of nature's oddest truths that most of us, especially young husbands, are ignorant of: The law of the Language of Love.

"Hey, come on, rise and be deeply impressed with your car's newfound beauty. I was . . ."

Kristy placed the article down next to her on the white couch and said, "I'm glad you had fun, but when you forget our plans to spend time together I feel bad, and right now I'm a little upset."

I was temporarily taken aback, "Plans?"

Then I remembered we had made plans to go to the café up our street that morning before the traffic and heat hit to try their breakfast and talk together. Our plan had been to sit for an hour or so and catch up on the week—something that Kristy loved to do.

There were problems with this plan that I had not seen during our conversation. One, I hate to sit. Two, sitting and talking on a Saturday morning were my least desirable options for that day. There were things to do! Three, I had failed to write down our date from the previous evening's conversation and thus had instantly forgotten it. And four, I was clueless as to the deeper issue here: How to tell Kristy that I love her *in a way she could hear?*

The first three issues mentioned were and are a matter of my hyperactivity. My short-term memory is still less than it should be, and I must write down commitments no matter how soon they are to take place. The intricacies of listening and enjoying the art of real conversation still elude me. The fourth issue is a matter known to all newlyweds. What I was about to discover in our conversation was that the first three were exacerbating the last and essential issue. I was attempting to tell my bride that I cared for her in ways that were akin not to her personality but to mine: activity, busyness, and tasks. "I love you, let me prove it by auto care, engaging in sports together, going on long adventures, runs, and hikes."

> I WAS ATTEMPTING TO TELL MY BRIDE THAT I CARED FOR HER IN WAYS THAT WERE AKIN NOT TO HER PERSONALITY BUT TO MINE.

What had yet to occur to me though was that my wife had her own language of love, and only she could teach it to me. I was about to take a crash course in Kristy's language. In condensed form our conversation that spring morning drove into my skull the need for a new set of skills. Kristy was about to inform me that if I wanted her to hear that I loved her, then I needed to hear her say it in the following way: "Jamie, listen to me. Let me talk without getting restless. Make time amid your projects to spend with me and occasionally do things that I want to do, like exploring new restaurants. Slow down long enough to become acquainted with my world and my emotions."

I am able to learn, and with my wife the motivation to learn is tremendous. But the task of learning her language had to be approached as a frontal assault upon my hyperactivity. Its drives and focus were diametrically opposed to her needs. It clouded the lessons I would have to learn to speak her language of love. The residue of the past was thick. I had always been able to drive myself through most challenges and lessons related to my learning difference. Now, within the intricate dance of this awesome relationship, I was going to have to learn new skills that were completely beyond both my comfort level and my past experience. I was going to have to learn to slow down and take leisure in conversation and loving.

IT IS FOR ALL LD INDIVIDUALS TO ANALYZE THE TYPE AND DEGREE OF THEIR OWN UNIQUE HURDLES AND THEN TO UNDERSTAND HOW THESE MIGHT AFFECT THEIR LOVED ONES.

I hate the very idea of slowing down, yet within that realm was my wife's heart and security. My adult hyperactivity affects me less academically than relationally. Kristy could not be blamed for confusing my restlessness in general with a lack of interest in her specifically.

The real world of loving intimacy demands that I rise above such confusing communications and tell her that since I love her, I will learn to sit and listen, to adjust to her verbal pacing instead of impatiently finishing her sentences for her, to more than feign interest, to really learn her speed and exult in our conversations. This is a two-way street, for she, too, must adapt to my frenetic pace, to climb Half Dome, to scuba dive, to have other adventures with me, and to do projects with abandon. The good news is that Kristy has a great deal of energy, too. I married a soulmate in this regard.

She is an athlete finely crafted in her outdoor skills and exuberant love of new challenges. Perhaps God, in part, designed her this way that I might have a fulfilling partner who understands a nonsedentary life.

It is for all LD individuals to analyze the type and degree of their own unique hurdles and then to understand how these might affect their loved ones. I call this "translation of impairment." I learn to translate the effects of my impairment into new arenas and situations. The tools of my past that were necessary for academic excellence now must be traded for new tools that are compatible with life as a married man. Obsessive discipline, hyperfocus on a project, and firm goals set on a daily basis must give way to a flexible schedule as my wife and children express their legitimate needs. My precious projects that were largely mechanical by nature have given way to more social tasks of building a home and secure environment for my growing family. These goals are less tangible, and their progress has fewer material benefits and rewards, yet they require my greatest attention.

I was able to be rigid and controlled in my unmarried past. Each day had a set beat and pace. It was predictable and thus controllable, especially emotionally. With my regimented exercise, work, and project schedule I could pretty well negate my roller-coaster emotional life and maintain a superficial demeanor even to my peers and colleagues.

No longer! Now I am a dad and a husband. Family, for me, means compromising for others' sake. Now my external controls must give way to real emotional centering and growth. I can't always get my rigid schedule up and running. Kids have their own needs, and I must be the parent, no longer the child. Thus this season of life has forced me to take the next step in my struggle with dyslexia.

Now I must teach myself to be less controlled and task oriented. What would happen if I only got one project done instead of seven? Will I be any less of a person if I work out only five times a week? I must lose some of the old rigidity of adolescence. Now I weigh actions beyond their immediate effect upon me, looking at their effect upon my loved ones. It's like juggling: How can I get time with my son, talk deeply with my wife, and meet my need for expelling the restlessness afflicting my legs all afternoon? *Take a long family walk, Jamie, and put your baby daughter in the backpack to make it a real workout.* I am slowly answering the call to consider the needs of others even as I attempt to meet my own. Parenting is a balancing act, and it has forced me into new growth. Struggling with a learning difference can be self-absorbing, even narcissistic. Now this selfishness, which was mandated by the degree of the battle itself, must change to a focus upon family.

> **KIDS HAVE THEIR OWN NEEDS, AND I MUST BE THE PARENT, NO LONGER THE CHILD.**

This has been deeply rewarding and stretching! I am discovering that life is designed to be more than self and that we are created by God to be more than victims who wrestle with their own issues. We can be intimately involved in the lives of others. Parenthood is awesome in this regard. It so frees us from the narrow and crippling regard for the all-important self. Here my me-generation meets its Waterloo and loses.

Perhaps the most intimate of all forms of human communication is prayer. There is a subtle art to its pacing, and its need for silence, passivity, and leisure. I include this in a chapter on marriage because of the Bible's many parallels between our relationship with the Creator and that of our most intimate earthly commitment. I am speaking here of more than just the shopping list of frenzied needs and crisis prayer. Prayer's deeper form of communion with our loving Creator is a listening for a still, small voice crying amid all the mundane traffic and anxious confusion of our busy minds.

My body is hyperactive. It detests stillness, as does my brain and soul. Images and ideas, fantasies and plans all sparkle and gleam, vying to attract my attention. My mind flits and jumps like St. Augustine's chained monkey who screamed and darted about while its leg was anchored to the floor. That great saint described his prayer mind as just like that monkey leaping from place to place, restless and active amid prayer's call for silence and stillness. If our

> IF OUR LIFE WITH CHRIST CAN BE LIKENED TO A MARRIAGE, THEN IT MUST BE THE BEST OF MARRIAGES WHERE TWO TALK INTIMATELY.

life with Christ can be likened to a marriage, then it must be the best of marriages where two talk intimately. I must listen to my Lord's quiet whispered voice, clearing the tangle of details that beg my attention and the urgent calls of my agenda. I am leagues from this discipline, and only occasionally do I truly enter a degree of spiritual stillness. Such alert passivity is foreign to my present vocabulary, but I hope to remedy that in its season.

He was a Jew, well acquainted with my Christian views and hyperactive ways. I am not accustomed to taking spiritual advice from Jews, except of course from a carpenter I know. But I was about to be taught a lesson about four thousand years of Jewish practice and its value. His brand of Judaism traced its roots all the way back to Abraham. And even though most of his day's work was as a psychologist, he had long since given wide sway to his Jewish and deeply spiritual musings in his advice to his patients. The doctor, whom I will call Steve, was about to ask me a question I had never been asked before.

"Jamie, how do you pray?" he asked, removing his glasses and closing his eyes after a long day with clients.

"Well, Steve, I pray to Jesus Christ." Here I figured I could get in a good note about my Lord; nothing wrong with a little evangelism on the side. But with a wave of the hand he dismissed the offhand attempt and bore in like a drill.

"That wasn't the question I asked, though nice try. No, not to whom, but rather how?" The glasses were back on and he was all focus and intensity. I described in detail my prayer routine: Adoration and praise start it off, then comes confession, followed by thanksgiving and finally supplication.

A wry smile spread across his well-lined face, and he let silence fill the room. "Have you forgotten anything?" he queried at last. I picked up some strange African artifact from his coffee table. Why did all shrinks have weird African tribal art adorning their walls and tables? Examining it, I stalled for time. From what I knew about Jewish prayer, I was at a loss for answers. Didn't they pray as I did? Same God, right?

"Who does all the talking in your prayers, Jamie?"

He got me. As I scanned my prayer habits, I saw activity, pacing, attempts at concentration, and inevitably a one-way conversation.

Years before I had heard stories of one of my ancestors

from Wales who had a prayer life vastly different from my own. His name was William. He was a coal miner's kid and an immigrant. He was poor, yet musical, and finally made good teaching the Bible after he graduated from a Chicago university. Perhaps it was the poverty or perhaps a deep humility, but he listened in prayer. I had been told that there would be long gaps in his prayers as he listened and mused on the silence. It was a conversation of sorts, an art form. As the years wore on, I imagine his silence grew while God's voice expanded until it finally enveloped the whole of the relationship. This is the stuff of still, small voices and of whispers and nuances. Not my forte, not yet at least.

If I want to be a better husband and father, and even more important, a man who loves God more deeply and trusts him more thoroughly, I will have to learn stillness, listening, and focus. This will require me to forget the compelling drives of my strange physiology and to a degree forget self long enough to be subsumed into another's world. This will require much further growth beyond.

As I have mentioned before, I was told, wrongly, as a child that I would grow out of my learning difference by the time I was eighteen. The truth of my experience is that no such thing happens. The battle and insights simply shift into new arenas of combat and therefore into new worlds to explore. I am one of the blessed few. I was diagnosed early and received tremendous support and education from a young age. Imagine all the millions of Americans who are not so blessed. Many as adults are only now receiving their initial diagnosis.

Motivation for this kind of battle is only a glance away. I see my son and wife drawing in his coloring book close by, and I know that they deserve a father and husband who is emotionally appropriate, balanced in his use of time and energy, able to listen as well as talk, capable of quiet moments as well as active projects, and available. They deserve a man who loves God humbly, who listens to and follows submissively his Lord. I have a long row to hoe yet in meeting this goal.

CHAPTER 16

Still Growing

The early March sun filtered through the still bare birch trees outside our New Jersey home. Melting patches of February snow dotted the lawn, but amidst the mud and ice, blades of new grass confidently pushed up. It was the end of a long winter, and I was ready to be an outdoorsman again. My wife, Kristy, sat on our couch with a mysterious glow about her. She greeted me with an outstretched hand as I returned home from a day at the office. A small plastic wand sat cradled in her palm. At first I didn't recognize the tiny device.

"Jamie, I have news for you." The way she said "news" was unique, filled with mystery and just a little hidden joy, as if some great secret were about to be revealed. I took the plastic stick in my hand and noticed that it was manufactured by Johnson & Johnson. On it was a double set of blue plus signs in tiny windows. "E.P.T." was stenciled on its flat handle. I was slow to comprehend what this was. Giggling, my wife of three years enlightened me. "Jamie, I'm pregnant." Those three words were about to change our lives in ways I certainly did not imagine and ways my wife did not dare expect.

We called our parents, celebrated with friends, and

were anxiously giddy. This child was desperately wanted
and eagerly prayed for.

Two weeks later my wife awoke with a start at four in
the morning. I felt her stir, cold air filling our bed as she
leapt out and dashed toward the bathroom. Ten minutes
later a shaking Kristy returned and lay down to snuggle
by my side. "Kristy, you're shivering!" I wrapped my arms
about her and tried to warm her up. "Are you all right?"
I could hear sobbing from the pillow in which her face
was buried, and her stomach felt tight and still heaving.

"Morning sickness." She moaned, drying her eyes and
turning toward me. "It'll pass as soon as I get some food
in my stomach."

But it didn't pass. It increased all that day. When I
returned from the office at day's end, I found her still in
bed and very pale. For the next five months my wife
would be racked with a rare condition called hyperemesis
(twenty-four-hour morning sickness that can endure for
months and do serious damage to pregnant women; in
extreme cases it can be fatal). My wife would be forced
to stay in bed and drink water in the form of ice chips
placed on the back of her tongue to trickle down her
throat. She would eat little and lose most of that instantly. During the first four months of pregnancy she
would drop thirty pounds, and she began her pregnancy
a very lean woman. She would suffer bone damage and
hair loss and be in constant fear of what might be happening to her baby. Would her near starvation affect this
unborn human being? Muscle tissue atrophied, and her
life was reduced to lying in bed fighting nausea so extreme that she bruised her ribs.

Little did we know that this was only a dress rehearsal
for her second pregnancy. During that time she would
suffer an even worse case of hyperemesis, be placed on
months of intravenous fluids, and be hospitalized repeatedly. In both these seasons of extreme testing and crisis

I learned two important lessons. First, I had married a very strong and courageous woman. She knew that there was a chance that her second pregnancy might bring a return of her torturing illness, yet she chose to attempt it anyway. What she received was indeed a worse case, yet throughout she never doubted the rightness of the act. She would bear our two glorious children, even if it very nearly killed her.

Kristy *will never* know how much I learned to love and cherish her character and determination during those dark seasons.

My second lesson was about me and my differences. During that time I lost my partner, my schedule that I so depended upon was smashed to smithereens, and I had to learn to be a caretaker for a very ill wife. During her second pregnancy, I had to care for her and our infant son. The hours of exercise, of working on projects, and of living a predictable home life were obliterated. Good sleep was infrequent. Responsibility for others was mounting. The core of self-focus in me had to die. The effects were immediate and clear.

My stuttering, long since vanquished, returned. Concentration lagged again, and my social ability, especially during times of intensity, eroded. My study times became unproductive as my distractibility roared. I was re-entering my old world. I was experiencing a de-evolution and learning that I had limits. I look back on this now and realize that I was being taught a marvelous lesson about my capabilities.

I have steep ambitions. My family has always and in various fields succeeded mightily. We rarely settle for mediocre, for halfway up the mountain, or for average. We drive for more. Yet in these twin illnesses I dipped into the pools of my emergency energy and found that when I push too hard I revert to my older self, a self I had no desire to resurrect.

Jogging down Elkwood Avenue in New Providence, New Jersey, I found myself becoming winded much more quickly than usual. A neighbor was watching my wife, allowing me to get a little free time. My wife was still very ill, but the doctor had high hopes of her turning a corner soon. I slowed to a walk in the afternoon heat of summer and pondered where my normally omnipresent energy had gone. Kristy had been sick the night before, and sleep had come for both of us only fitfully. I was now operating on about four hours' rest, and the previous few nights hadn't been much better. I was tired to the bone and was discovering for the first time in my life what exhausted meant. My work at the church was at best fair. I had little patience for the arduous process of writing new classes for each week's teaching of Bible classes. I was moody and my speech, especially before the congregation, was full of stammers and raced at over two hundred words a minute.

I DIPPED INTO THE POOLS OF MY EMERGENCY ENERGY AND FOUND THAT WHEN I PUSH TOO HARD I REVERT TO MY OLD SELF.

Somewhere in the back of my hopes was a scene of my future: I would be a pastor of a large church, oversee bold ministries, and lead a sizable staff. I would travel and speak, just as my ancestors had, and write numerous books. I would climb the tall steeples and make a name for myself alongside the other greats of my clan. As I stumbled back from my discouraging run down Elkwood, I saw for the first time how dangerous my dreams were, for I was not wired for the kind of lifestyle that such dreams would demand. Simply keeping my therapeutic schedule of good diet, strong exercise, and simple lifestyle would drain much of the precious energies needed to charge into my ambitions. Yet if I did not remain diligently disciplined in my habits, I would revert as I was now during this season of crisis to my old unremediated self. That old self could not spell correctly, let alone climb tall steeples of ministerial fame. I could hear the Holy Spirit cheering in the background of my soul that at last I understood that if I were ever to be used to minister to large numbers, it would be by God's providence and not my own abilities.

It is a shocking moment when the boy finally dies in the man, and we see ourselves without our childish and vain ambitions, but rather as we actually are. I sat down on an old gravestone in the tree-lined cemetery across the woods from my house and pondered what this realization was all about. The graveyard was of the old style, planted with varying sizes of monuments depending upon an individual's pocketbook and their family's esteem. Some were grand and many were simple, but all had felt the ravages of the years, and the inscriptions were hard to read due to the worn stone work. I laughed as I saw one of the larger monuments now being slowly tipped sideways by the root of a young sapling. It would not be long before the tree had destroyed it. Many of these people had been famous in their era, but now all were equally forgotten by time and equally cared for by God. Graveyards are a good place to evaluate human ambitions. The chuckle in me grew into laughter. My ambitions weren't worthy of the deterioration of life that I and my family would experience if I were to expend my resources in the pursuit of my ego's hopes.

I am now in a season of realistic assessment of what is a healthy and sustainable ambition amidst my limitations. Kristy's illnesses served to simulate the kind of frenetic pace such ambitions would demand. I did not like the outcome of that experience, for I saw myself to be all too mortal, normal, and limited. But I would have been a fool to ignore these expensively purchased conclusions.

Seven months into Kristy's first pregnancy, I walked home and smelled a strange odor coming from our kitchen. Food was cooking. I dashed across the backyard, threw open the door, and stood dumbfounded in the hall. My pregnant yet emaciated wife was up, and even more surprising had gone out shopping and was up to her elbows in taco fixings. What would have sent her into severe nausea just twenty-four hours before was now being eagerly prepared.

> I AM NOW IN A SEASON OF REALISTIC ASSESSMENT OF WHAT IS A HEALTHY AND SUSTAINABLE AMBITION.

"Are you doing what I think you are?" I asked with some disbelief.

She turned and looked at me. She didn't need to answer. Her lips and chin told the whole story. Guacamole smeared her lips, and a fleck of onion was pressed on her chin. She had been tasting the dinner with some eagerness, and she was now opening up hot salsa. "How does pizza sound for tomorrow's dinner?" she replied, so full of grateful release that she almost dropped the salsa jar just getting the words out.

The next two months brought feasting and togetherness. I had my partner back, and we made the most of it! Pizza and Japanese food, movies and popcorn, long walks and, as winter descended again, evening strolls through the leaf piles that dotted our small town.

The night of December 5 brought a halt to all of this. Our son was eager to arrive. Labor began tenuously and then exploded. By seven the next morning I watched my boy enter the world in what can only be described as a miracle birth, so mundane yet so awesome. It is the custom in New Jersey and perhaps in other states to allow the father to cut the umbilical cord. (That is about all the really hard work I did compared to my much overworked wife and the doctors in the whole process.) As I prepared to make the cut, I was overwhelmed by a wave of love for this boy. It felt as if a new chamber of my heart had been created just for him, with no diminishing of the love I held for my wife or for my Lord. The increase in such loving capacity actually physically hurt at that moment. I also felt as if I would die for this boy instantly if the need ever arose. There was this sacrificial quality to it that I had not expected—protective, passionate, and huge! I cut the cord.

For a moment nothing happened, and I wondered if I had done something wrong. Then I watched as two things simultaneously occurred in that cramped room: My son, just seconds old turned blue, a deep ghastly color that bespoke horrors of suffocation and death. My son couldn't breathe! Before my eyes he was dying. At the same moment a nurse pushed a large red button on the wall next to me and in moments a crew from the neonatal ICU charged in and whisked my boy away from Kristy and me. I followed in a daze. I was helpless to do anything but look on as my boy was placed in an oxygen-filled incubator, struggling to breathe and with mouth wide open trying to scream.

Hoses were placed down his throat and finally the child's lungs were cleared enough for him to utter a room-piercing wail. I have never heard such a beautiful sound in all my life, for his terror had turned to anger and he was screaming and fussing up a powerful storm.

With limbs flying in all directions, his once-blue color turned into a rage-filled crimson. The medical staff on the unit looked up at me and beamed.

They explained that Nathan, our newborn son, had winter baby syndrome, a condition of too much fluid in the lungs. Yet he was healthy and his lungs were now clear. My wife cradled him in her tired arms full of relief and gratitude.

I will never forget that morning's terror. The thought of our son suffering was a visceral ripping of our very beings. The realization soon arrived that I had another issue to be aware of that might cause him damage. Would my boy (and later his sister, Kelly) be afflicted with a learning difference?

There is a quiet watchfulness in my wife and myself. We look for cues, for if being a learning-differenced person is ever a blessing, it is always first through hardship that that blessing is realized. I would prefer that my children be blessed in other ways. Yet the genetic history of my family is clear—we are prone to this sort of challenge. I want to protect them from those struggles and hurts. I want them to be happy and have easy, free childhoods with such lessons reserved for the future and for adulthood. I am a typical parent in this. Yet my attitude is also troublesome.

For years I have watched protective parents attempting to shield their children from that which would make them grow and deepen. I have told stories in this book about parents who protect too much and thus retard the remediation process for the LD student, which always begins with struggle. Parenthood has brought such a sea of emotions and cares that I can see how clear the temptation is to insulate our children from threats. But how could we ever keep them from a disability that is from within? Their characters will be forged in fire should they be so afflicted and perhaps so blessed.

As I've studied the lives of famous people with learning disabilities, I've seen the common denominator of iron characters: General George Patton, Bruce Jenner, Albert Einstein, Greg Louganis, Thomas Edison, John D. Rockefeller, to name but a few. And who is to say that their genius in their own particular fields was not born from the fire of such struggle? How many times I have been told that potted plants don't survive out of doors! Too much protection and my children, if so afflicted, will never be able to thrive under their learning difference's tutelage. This is a bitter lesson for a protective father. One more issue to be surrendered to God.

"I was sure that just two hours ago I vacuumed and straightened up," I thought to myself in resignation. My wife and I for the ten thousandth time since our children were born shook our heads and wondered how we could be outnumbered when we only had two small kids! About us was strewn the wreckage: toys lay everywhere, graham crackers were ground into the white carpet, and juice boxes littered the tables. The place was a mess.

My thirteen-month-old daughter, Kelly, clung to my leg begging to be picked up, while Nate shouted to me and Kristy that he wanted to play chase. This would be the seventeenth game of chase this morning, and he was getting fast! Diaper bags were strategically placed in every car, the room had been baby proofed years before, while fences and gates guarded each staircase and doorway. My wife and I are normally fastidious, neat to an extreme, and orderly people. At least we used to be.

I have always prided myself on a routine and schedule that prioritizes getting tasks done—the hard ones first and the play left as a reward. Cars are kept properly maintained, and the garage was arranged rightly for a mechanic's paradise. This used to be my world of pre-dictable pacing. Before children my learning-differenced world was guarded by these walls of order and precision.

Now I can barely remember such days. We race to keep ahead of the chaos. By nightfall we are often behind the curve. Time for fastidious attitudes of the past is now eagerly given up to the two little bundles of needs and joy. Our order's demise was well spent on these gifts of human rambunctiousness. Slowly I am changing. Mess is okay; lots of crumbs and only a few projects, a crazed schedule, even interrupted sleep—all are becoming acceptable for the greater priority of being parents.

PERHAPS WITH CHILDREN CAME THE CONFIDENCE WITHIN THAT ALLOWED THE OLD RIGIDITY TO BE BLOWN TO SMITHEREENS BY THESE BOUNCING BUNDLES.

I see growth here away from the rigid world of schedule and emotional control that my old discipline used to exert upon my inner world. Perhaps with children came the confidence within that allowed the old rigidity to ease or to be blown to smithereens by these bouncing bundles. The self-focus of the disabled man has given way to the parent who spends much of his time investing in other lives and in the future. Such giving that my wife and I do goes a long way in taming the inner storms of energy and hyperactive swings.

Perhaps when the children are grown and independent, we will return to our more predictable ways, rigid neatness and clean rugs, but we won't have to. I now have options and a variety of tools to use in controlling the sine curve of my inner world. I love getting older! My thirties have certainly bested my twenties by leagues in the joy and growth department. This is due in large part to the birth of my children and to marriage to Kristy. If my goal was to grow up and mature, then having children was just the means I needed to drive me to that point.

My learning difference has been such a teacher! As I age, I see new opportunities and options. One set of tools is exchanged for another, while growth is directed into whole new arenas. Marriage and children have catapulted me into a marvelous season and dimension. Flexibility grows, and a quiet confidence and deep joy unencumbered by schedule take root. If this is what growing older is all about, then I relish the passage of years.

I may never be able to write a conclusion for this book. I may always have to confront bits of my LD, even in the years ahead. But I must not avoid the pain of struggling with those challenges. It is through facing such pain that I will grow. Those of us with learning disorders must keep in mind that we are fortunate to have been chosen for the privilege of fighting our battles. God would not have given us the disorder if he did not also intend to give us the resources to combat it.

Those of us who have such disabilities will see evidence of God's providence and rich grace that other people may not even dream exist. Through our pain we will gain sensitivity and through our struggle we will be taught discipline, and if there comes a time when we can no longer fight the battle on our own—as I found at Wooster—then we will learn one of the greatest lessons of all: dependence on God and on committed relationships will carry us through.

When it comes to forming a truly intimate relationship, I have one role model: Jesus Christ. He accepts me unconditionally and in spite of my fears of rejection. He makes no effort to control me or our relationship; we are bound by mutual love and regard. It's going to take me some time to follow his example, but I can't think of anything better to do with my life. I trust him, even with my fears and apprehensions. I know now that he will never let me go.

At times I offend him and he reacts in righteous anger. He confronts the wrong I have done, yet he never stops loving me. At those times when I make him proud by accepting his will over my own, he commends me, but he makes it clear that my obedience is not the reason why he loves me. It does me no good to argue that I am too dumb to be loved, nor can I claim that any kind of achievement has earned me his love. He simply does love. And that is the way I want to relate. That is the way I want to win the final struggle against a disability that has become—in an amazing sense—a blessing.